HANDBOOK

for Advisors of
Career and Technical
Student Organizations

5th Edition

Rosco C. Vaughn
Paul R. Vaughn
Lanette D. Vaughn

The American Association for Vocational Materials (AAVIM) is a nonprofit association comprised of American universities, colleges and divisions of career and technical education. AAVIM's mission is to prepare, publish and distribute quality instructional materials for more effective teaching and learning. Direction of the organization is provided by representation from member states and agencies. AAVIM also works with teacher organizations, government agencies and industry to provide excellence in instructional materials.

AAVIM Staff

Gary Farmer	Director
Kim Butler	Business Manager
Dean Roberts	Shipping Supervisor
Vicki J. Eaton	Art Director/
	Production Coordinator

**Handbook for Advisors of
Career and Technical Student Organizations**

Fifth Edition Editorial Staff

Katie Carey	Technical Writer/Editor

Copyright 2007 by the American Association for Vocational Instructional Materials, 220 Smithonia Road, Winterville, Georgia 30683-9527.

For information about other AAVIM instructional materials, to place an order or request a free catalog, please write or contact:

AAVIM
220 Smithonia Rd.
Winterville, Georgia 30683-9527
Phone: (706) 742-5355
Fax: (706) 742-7005
1-800-228-4689
Website: www.aavim.com

ISBN: 0-89606-386-0
Printed in the United States of America

Author, Fifth Edition

Rosco C. Vaughn is Professor and Credentialing Coordinator for the Department of Animal Sciences and Agricultural Education at California State University, Fresno where he is actively engaged in training future teachers of agricultural education. He is responsible for the changes seen in this fifth edition.

Editorial Staff - Previous Editions

First Edition
Paul R. Vaughn, Rosco C. Vaughn, and Lanette D. Vaughn are responsible for the original manuscript as well as proofing of the finished copy for completeness and accuracy.

Donna Prichett was the editor and art director for the first edition. She is credited with the original illustrations.

Second Edition, Third Edition
Paul R. Vaughn authored changes to the second and third editions. George W. Smith acted as editor.

Fourth Edition
Paul R. Vaughn authored changes to the fourth edition. He was also responsible for obtaining and updating photographs used in the fourth edition.

Acknowledgements

AAVIM and the author are grateful for the cooperation of organizations and individuals in the revision of this handbook. The logos of the various student career and technical organizations seen on the cover and within this publication are used with permission. Their use and other material provided does not imply any endorsement by any individual or organization of the information presented within this publication.

TABLE OF CONTENTS

CAREER AND TECHNICAL STUDENT ORGANIZATION ADVISOR'S CREED

I Believe In Career and Technical Education - I teach it by choice and not by chance. I believe in the ability of career and technical education to develop better, more useful citizens; and I am convinced of its necessity in a democratic society.

I Believe That Career and Technical Student Organizations Are An Integral Part Of Career and Technical Education; that they are essential to a career and technical student's education, as such, I will do everything within my power to ensure that my students' leadership and personal skills are developed to the same degree as their technical skills.

I Believe That Career and Technical Student Organization Activities Should Be Designed By The Students For The Students, and that my major function as advisor is to assist and guide students in developing and constructing such activities. It is my duty to structure the activities so that they build the characteristics of cooperation, leadership, citizenship, and patriotism.

I Believe That My Leadership Role Is Of Utmost Importance in demonstrating to students the skills that they will need to become effective members of today's American society. Therefore, I will strive to set the highest personal moral and professional standards possible.

I Believe In The Worth Of The Individual; that every student is important. I shall not neglect the student who falls behind or the one that speeds ahead. I shall never knowingly hinder the education of any student, and I shall strive to provide the opportunity for every student to gain recognition through participation in my career and technical student organization.

I Believe In Career and Technical Student Organizations and in their ability to improve the individual. I shall continually endeavor to improve my skills as an advisor and shall never, despite temptations to the contrary, deny my students access to this essential educational ingredient. I proudly accept my responsibilities as a career and technical education teacher and advisor - I shall not fail in either responsibility.

Introduction

Welcome to the world of career and technical education! The authors presuppose that the reader already is familiar with the field and seeks to learn more about the role of the career and technical education (CTE) teacher; specifically, serving as an advisor for a career and technical student organization (CTSO).

The Handbook for Advisors of Career and Technical Student Organizations provides a summary for the ten CTSOs recognized by the U.S. Department of Education. While a comprehensive background and history for each CTSO can easily be found within websites or other promotional material, the Handbook acquaints the reader with the responsibilities of an advisor and provides detailed information that will help fulfill these responsibilities.

The authors hope that this book will improve the educational experience teachers provide CTE students. Study of the Handbook will reveal that CTE activities are essential to students' overall education. Activities are organized and conducted by students, and the advisor is responsible for assistance and supervision.

The Handbook consists of twelve chapters. The first describes the unique relationship between CTSOs and CTE programs; the remaining chapters cover eleven major responsibilities of an advisor.

Note the several general terms are used throughout the Handbook. "CTE" is used to denote career and technical education, 'CTSO" to denote the CTSO's local chapter, club, or branch in a particular school.

An education program is only as effective as its instructor; similarly, a CTSO is only as effective as its advisor. The Handbook is written with the goal that it will improve the ability of instructors to capably and proficiently advise CTSOs. The spirit of the book is best expressed by 'The Career and Technical Student Organization Advisor's Creed" developed by the authors.

CHAPTER 1
Relationship of CTSOs to the Total CTE Program

How do CTSOs fit into the education program? Can a CTE teacher spend classroom time on CTSO activities? What are a teacher's responsibilities in regard to a CTSO? An educator must answer these questions before he or she can prepare an instructional program. This section answers these and other questions regarding the unique status of CTSOs within the U.S. educational system.

Note this important distinction. Unlike other student clubs or activities, the CTSO is not separate from or optional to the educational program. Rather it is vital to the education program, providing students with unique training.

Only a CTE teacher can serve as an advisor of a CTSO chapter. The advisor's and instructor's roles are one and the same: each is an integral part of the other, and neither exists by itself. Responsibilities of a CTSO advisor, and the relationship of the CTSO to the education program, are discussed under these headings:

▶   The integral relationship of CTSOs

▶   The value of CTSOs

▶   The relationship between the CTE instructor and the CTSO advisor

1. THE INTEGRAL RELATIONSHIP OF CTSOs

The term *integral* describes a relationship that is necessary for completeness; when one item is described as having an integral relationship with another, it suggests that each is such an essential part of the other that neither could be considered complete by itself. This indicates that CTE programs are incomplete without CTSOs, and the CTSOs cannot exist unless they are included within the instructional programs.

Federal law recognizes this integral relationship. Amendments to Congress' Vocational Education Act of 1963 authorized Federal funds for states' CTSO activities that are described in state plans, included as an integral part of a CTE program, and supervised by qualified staff. This legislation defined *integral part* as:

▶   *Training* in an organized educational program that prepares individuals for paid or unpaid employment in a career requiring other than a baccalaureate or higher degree;

▶   *Field or laboratory work* incidental to CTE training; or

▶   *Development and acquisition* of instructional materials, supplies, and equipment for instructional services.

The legislation emphasized that CTSOs are an important part of the total instructional program in CTE, and an essential ingredient in preparing young people for the world of work. The Federal definition clarified the relationship of CTSOs in regard to a total educational program, and helped provide the basis for the diagram in Figure 1-1. The diagram illustrates that the instructional program is made up of three overlapping parts: classroom instruction, laboratory instruction (often including "hands-on" occupational experience in a real-life setting), and CTSO activities. Though each is a distinct part of CTE, all three are essential, so intertwined that they cannot be fully separated if a complete

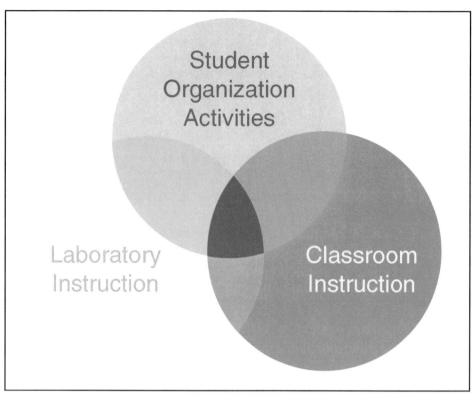

Figure 1-1. The relationship of student organizations to the total career and technical education program.

program is to be offered. Thus teachers can and should spend classroom time on CTSO activities. To do otherwise neglects an important part of a student's CTE.

Another way to understand the relationship between the CTSO and the CTE program is to compare their activities with those of other school organizations. Activities are often categorized into two types: extracurricular and intracurricular. *Extracurricular* activities take place outside of a program of instruction; though they may be related to a particular subject, they are not part of a planned instructional program and are not incorporated into a lesson plan or curriculum. *Intracurricular* activities are incorporated into the instruction program and receive classroom time; more than a social aspect of the school, they are considered a necessary part of the student's education.

Though extracurricular activities are more widespread, CTSOs are uniquely intracurricular in nature. While a varsity team coach who also teaches physical education would be questioned if he or she were to coach the team during class, a CTE teacher would instead be questioned if he or she spent no class time discussing CTSOs. The varsity team is an extracurricular activity with no place in the curriculum; CTSOs have a definite part in the curriculum and are used to promote skills necessary to gain employment in a field.

From the very beginning of CTE, CTSOs have been recognized by Federal legislators as a vital part of instruction. Five significant acts are discussed below.

▸ The ***Smith-Hughes Act of 1917***, sponsored by Senator Hoke Smith and Rep. Dudley Hughes (both of Georgia), provided Federal funds for teaching agriculture, trades, industry, and home economics in secondary schools and stipulated the career and technical character of courses to be taught. Though it did not specifically mention them, Smith-Hughes provided the foundation for the first CTSOs.

▶ The *"George Acts"* were a series of bills cosponsored by Senator Walter F. George of Georgia that supplemented and continued Smith-Hughes. The ***George-Reed Act of 1929*** provided additional financial support for teaching agriculture and home economics, and to hire subject matter specialists. The ***George-Ellzey Act of 1934*** and the ***George-Dean Act of 1936*** increased funding for agriculture, home economics, and trade and industrial education. The ***George-Barden Act***, also known as the Vocational Education Act of 1946, authorized funds for teachers associated with Future Farmers of America (FFA) and the New Farmers of America.

▶ ***Public Law 740***, passed in 1950, provided a Federal charter for FFA. It recognized the integral relationship between CTSOs and instructional programs, and authorized employees of the US Office of Education (now the U.S. Department of Education) to work with CTSOs. Public Law 740 established a pattern of treating CTSOs as an essential component of CTE. Congress in 1998 reviewed and passed technical amendments to Public Law 740; these revisions are included in Public Law 105-225, the current charter legislation for FFA.

▶ The ***Vocational Education Act of 1963*** replaced much of Smith-Hughes. It increased Federal support for CTE schools and work-study programs, did away with specific occupational categories, and supported research and training. Subsequent amendments in 1968 and 1976 provided specific definitions for elements of CTE instruction, including integral CTSOs.

▶ The ***Carl D. Perkins Vocational Education Acts of 1984, 1990, and 1998*** (the Perkins Acts) provide the basis for today's CTE program. Named for Rep. Carl D. Perkins of Kentucky, the acts seek to improve the quality of career and technical training, modernize programs, and expand access. The 1990 Act provided cooperative academic links between secondary and post-secondary institutions, while the 1998 Act focused on developing challenging academic standards and accountability. The Perkins Acts continue the policy of allowing states to use Federal funds for CTSOs in secondary and post-secondary institutions.

Figure 1-2. Our nation's leaders have long recognized that CTSOs are an essential component of career and technical education. Photo courtesy of the National FFA Organization.

In addition, the U.S. Department of Education adopted a policy in 1990 supporting the integral role of CTSOs within the educational system. The policy recognized the ten major CTSOs, facilitated services to help CTSOs work with state agencies, and endorsed the use of Federal and state funds for CTSO activities. Many state Departments of Education have since adopted similar policies. The US Department of Education's most recent policy is provided in the Appendix.

The National Association of State Directors of Vocational Technical Education Consortium has also provided support for CTSOs. This organization adopted a policy in 1996 supporting ten major CTSOs; a copy of this policy as revised in 1999 is also provided in the Appendix.

2. THE VALUE OF CTSOs

Former members provide the best assessment of any CTSO's strengths. These summarize the comments frequently given by past participants in CTSOs:

▶ CTSOs *create interest*. Former members often mention that CTSOs, not classes, led them into CTE: providing participants with information about specific occupations and the educational programs related to them. Wise teachers recognize CTSOs as an effective recruitment tool.

▶ CTSOs *develop both leadership and "followship" skills*. Participants learn a valuable lesson in democracy: members, not just leaders, enable a group to reach its goals. They also learn that leadership is a learned ability, not one that occurs naturally. CTSOs provide opportunities to participate in leadership situations similar to those encountered in later life.

▶ CTSOs *develop confidence and positive attitudes*. Young people are at a critical point in their lives: establishing identities and facing new responsibilities, yet without being treated fully as adults. Successful advisors recognize that CTSOs provide opportunities for gaining greater self-assurance and a more affirming outlook.

▶ CTSOs *promote group activity*. They provide a structure within which participants learn to work with others: one that promotes essential qualities of tolerance, inclusion, understanding, and cooperation.

▶ CTSOs *promote initiative*. As democratic groups, CTSOs encourage participation and reward individual enterprise. Each member is given as much responsibility as he or she seeks; there are few limits to a member's goals and aspirations.

▶ CTSOs *encourage and vitalize students*. Education should be enjoyable and motivating. Many former members relate that CTSOs heightened their interest in education, thus encouraging them to stay in school. A CTSO is an effective motivational tool.

▶ CTSOs *help support occupational experience programs*. National CTSOs spend millions of dollars each year to reward members who participate in occupational experience programs. This show of support for these programs enables many to improve and expand their occupational skills.

- CTSOs *develop occupational competencies and social abilities*. A major goal of a CTE program is to prepare individuals for employment in a particular field. CTSOs provide job-specific activities that build core competencies as well as important social skills.

- CTSOs *promote self-improvement and scholarship*. CTSOs help participants identify a use for the skills they develop, often for the first time. This insight often provides an incentive for participants to study harder and improve their abilities.

- CTSOs *provide individual recognition*. Everyone has a recognition need: CTSOs help participants meet these needs in a constructive way. This is perhaps one of the greatest benefits of participation.

Employers "purchase the product" created by CTE programs, so naturally they have important views about the quality of the product delivered. Employers affirm their support of CTSOs by donating millions of dollars each year to education programs. Many national corporations and state associations have established foundations to collect and administer these funds.

Figure 1-4. Participation in CTSO activities helps students develop confidence. Photo courtesy of FBLA-PBL, Inc.

Figure 1-5. Teamwork and cooperation are skills that are emphasized by CTSOs. Photo courtesy of the National FFA Organization.

5

Figure 1-6. Participants are rewarded for developing initiative and responsibility through participation in CTSO activities. Photo courtesy of DECA Inc.

Figure 1-7. Many CTSO members participate in skills competitive events to master the skills needed to enter the nation's workforce. Photo courtesy of SkillsUSA Inc.

Employers show their support in other ways as well: they continually reaffirm their approval of the skills developed by CTSOs, and are more likely to hire participants. Employers remind CTE educators that they want employees who:

▸ Work well with others.

▸ Are dependable.

▸ Show an interest in the company's field.

▸ Can lead as well as follow.

▸ Demonstrate tolerance and understanding.

▸ Display initiative and accept responsibility.

Note too that employers often place at least as much emphasis on these skills as they do on technical abilities. Former members confirm that they developed these skills through participation in CTSOs.

Figure 1-8. CTSO participation provides opportunities for members to develop their social skills. Photo courtesy of TSA.

Figure 1-9. CTSOs enhance members' scholarship skills and promote self-improvement. Photo courtesy of Business Professionals of America.

Figure 1-10. Employers make significant contributions to CTSOs, donating millions of dollars to the organizations each year. Many employers also participate on boards that direct or guide the CTSOs. Photo courtesy of the National PAS Organization.

Research related to the value of CTSOs is somewhat limited, due to the difficulty of isolating and measuring the effects attributed to membership. Two major findings, however, clearly emphasize the value of CTSOs:

▸ *Former members continually rate the skills learned in CTSOs as very important and extremely helpful in later life.* They list citizenship, cooperation, leadership, tolerance, dependability, and initiative, and state that these were developed through participation in the CTSOs.

▸ *A majority of workers lose their jobs because of poor interpersonal skills, rather than a lack of technical competence.* Job retention is equally as important a goal of CTE as is job placement. Several studies show that employees lose their jobs because they can't get along with others. CTSOs provide opportunities to work together toward a common goal, which may be the single most important skill in a future job market.

3. THE RELATIONSHIP BETWEEN THE INSTRUCTOR AND THE CTSO ADVISOR

Though the two roles are distinct, there is no difference between a CTE instructor and a CTSO advisor: they are one and the same person. A CTE instructor functions as a classroom teacher, a coordinator, and an advisor. Indeed, one function is not complete if the others are not performed.

Part of the task of teaching includes the development of students' leadership and personal qualities that will enable them to obtain and retain a job. Teaching only technical information while ignoring leadership and personal development is not an effective, responsible approach.

Figure 1-11. The role of the advisor cannot be separated from that of the teacher. Both roles facilitate learning.
Photo courtesy of the National FFA Organization..

The basic responsibility of every CTE instructor and advisor is to integrate the CTSO into the educational program. The instructor/advisor can encourage all students to become members. He or she can include units of instruction on the CTSO and its activities in the curriculum. He or she can incorporate the CTSO into appropriate classroom or laboratory instructional programs. Most importantly, however, he or she can accept responsibilities for advising and supervising CTSO activities. These include:

▸ *Orienting potential members to the fundamentals and principles of the CTSO.* The advisor must know the history and philosophy of the CTSO, and must develop and utilize a lesson plan to instruct students about it. He or she also needs to orient students to the CTSO's history, philosophy, rules, and principles, and be able to enroll new members in the CTSO.

▸ *Supervising the development, publication, and implementation of an annual Program of Activities (POA).* An annual plan identifies the activities necessary to help the CTSO meet the personal and occupational needs of its members. The advisor must help develop the plan and facilitate efforts to carry it out.

- ▸ ***Supervising the election and training of chapter officers.*** The advisor must ensure that chapter officers are elected in a democratic manner and are familiar with their duties and responsibilities. He or she also needs to provide the officers with additional training, to help them provide effective chapter leadership.

- ▸ ***Preparing members for participation in local, district, state, and national activities.*** One of the most enjoyable aspects of CTSO membership is participating in functions at all organizational levels. The advisor must be familiar with these functions and provide members with the background information and training necessary to participate.

- ▸ ***Helping members advance within the available degrees of the CTSO.*** Many CTSOs develop various degrees of membership to signify advancement and greater accomplishment. The advisor is responsible to help members advance within these degrees. He or she must be familiar with the qualifications and requirements for each degree, and convey that information to all members.

- ▸ ***Supervising the development and activities of a public relations program.*** A successful CTSO establishes and maintains a good public image. The advisor must understand the key factors involved in developing the CTSO's image, and assist members to put these into operation.

- ▸ ***Supervising the chapter's financial operation and fund-raising activities.*** An active local chapter may handle thousands of dollars a year. The advisor must help members earn enough money to finance the year's activities, and ensure that funds collected are recorded and disbursed appropriately. He or she must also see that state and national dues are collected and submitted according to organizational rules.

- ▸ ***Helping members develop and conduct award and recognition programs.*** CTSOs recognize members who complete outstanding accomplishments. The advisor must help facilitate an annual awards program or banquet, allowing other students and community members to acknowledge exceptional members.

- ▸ ***Providing instruction for members in leadership and personal development.*** An important aspect of a CTSO is the development of leadership and personal skills that help members become effective participants in society. The advisor must be able to teach leadership and personal development skills, and encourage students to participate.

- ▸ ***Ensuring that students with special needs are included in the chapter.*** Students with special needs receive a particular benefit from participation in a CTSO. The advisor must ensure that provisions are made to enable all students to participate, utilizing their talents and abilities to the fullest.

- ▸ ***Supervising a yearly evaluation of the chapter.*** The advisor must help members determine whether organizational goals have been met. Chapter awards are an effective way for a local CTSO to be evaluated in comparison with others in the state or nation, and thus to improve going forward.

CTE teachers who perform these tasks satisfactorily are effective advisors, and provide a complete educational program. The ***Handbook*** is structured to help the advisor perform each of these responsibilities.

NOTES

CHAPTER 2
Orienting Students to the Fundamentals and Principles of the CTSO

New students to a CTE program need to be oriented to the history, philosophy, and purpose of the corresponding CTSO. They must become familiar with the CTSO's activities before they can take an active part: seeing value in participation and understanding the benefits of membership. Students will more readily "buy in" to an organization when they understand its purpose and the relevance of its activities.

The advisor needs to orient students to the fundamentals and principles of the CTSO. Four essential tasks are discussed below:

1. History and philosophy of CTSOs

2. Lesson plan to teach the fundamentals of the CTSO

3. Orienting students to the operation of the chapter

4. Enrolling members into the CTSO

1. HISTORY AND PHILOSOPHY OF CTSOs

The advisor needs to become familiar with background information about relevant CTSOs: official manuals, handbooks, and websites are good sources of information. The following summaries are a brief introduction to the purposes and principles of ten major CTSOs; more detailed information (e.g., organizational creeds, colors, and mottos) can be found in the Appendix.

The CTSOs, listed in order of their establishment, are:

- FFA
- Future Business Leaders of America – Phi Beta Lambda (FBLA)
- Family, Career and Community Leaders of America (FCCLA)
- DECA
- SkillsUSA
- Technology Student Association (TSA)
- Business Professionals of America (BPA)
- Health Occupations Students of America (HOSA)
- National Postsecondary Agricultural Student Organization (PSA)
- National Young Farmer Educational Association (NYFA)

▸ **FFA**

National FFA Headquarters Operation
1410 King Street, Suite 400
Alexandria, VA 22314
703-838-5889

National FFA Center
6060 FFA Drive, PO Box 68960
Indianapolis, IN 46268-0960
317-802-6060
www.ffa.org

Figure 2-1. The official FFA emblem. Used by permission.

FFA is the national organization for students enrolled in agricultural education programs. Members prepare for more than 300 careers including agriculture science, technology development, marketing, engineering, production agriculture, horticulture, and forestry. FFA's mission is to create a positive difference in students' lives by developing their potential for premier leadership, personal growth, and career success through agricultural education.

Future Farmers of America began in Kansas City, MO in 1928 and is the oldest CTSO in the US. Patterned after the Future Farmers of Virginia, it sought to provide leadership and competitive activities for farm boys. In 1950 the FFA received a Federal charter when Congress passed Public Law 81-740 (see *Chapter 1: Relationship of CTSOs to the Total CTE Program*). The organization included members from off-farm agricultural programs in 1963; merged in 1965 with the New Farmers of America, an organization for African-American students; and included female members in 1969.

In 1988 delegates voted to change the official name from the Future Farmers of America to the National FFA Organization. The name change reflected FFA's evolution in response to expanded agricultural opportunities encompassing science, business, and technology.

FFA's organizational structure consists of chartered state associations, each comprised of local chapters. Schools may also have "mini-chapters" representing different agricultural programs (e.g., horticulture, mechanics, and production agriculture). Members hold office at local, state, and national levels. The national FFA president, secretary, and four vice presidents represent the membership to officials in agriculture, education, and government. State and chapter officers work with advisors to plan and conduct activities for members and to carry out local chapter or state association business. Chapter and state student offices include a president, vice-president, secretary, treasurer, reporter, and sentinel.

FFA offers four kinds of membership. *Active* members are students enrolled in agricultural education. *Alumni* members are former active members, professional educators, parents, and others supportive of the organization. *Collegiate* chapter members are students enrolled in agricultural courses at postsecondary institutions. *Honorary* members are those who have rendered outstanding service to agricultural education and FFA.

▶ **Future Business Leaders of America – Phi Beta Lambda**

Future Business Leaders of
America – Phi Beta Lambda
1912 Association Drive
Reston, VA 20191-1591
800-325-2946
www.fbla-pbl.org
general@fbla.org

Figure 2-2. The official FBLA-PBL emblem. Used by permission.

Future Business Leaders of America – Phi Beta Lambda (FBLA-PBL) is the national association for junior high, middle, intermediate, high school, and postsecondary students interested in careers in business or business-related fields. The organization's mission is to bring business and education together in a positive working relationship, through innovative leadership and career development programs.

FBLA was first developed in 1937 at Columbia University in New York. In 1940, the National Council for Business Education officially sponsored the organization. The first high-school chapter was organized in 1942, the first postsecondary chapter was chartered in 1958, and middle school chapters were added in 1994.

FBLA-PBL is comprised of four divisions: FBLA for high school students; FBLA Middle Level for junior high, middle, and intermediate school students; PBL (founded in 1958) for postsecondary students; and the Professional Division, for individuals supporting the goals of business education.

FBLA-PBL offers two kinds of membership. *Active* members are students who participate in business or related fields in the three student divisions. ***Professional Division*** members are persons associated with or participating in FBLA-PBL's organizational development (e.g., a business advisory council) in the Professional Division.

Figure 2-3. State and national FBLA-PBL meetings provide members with recognition for outstanding accomplishments. Photo courtesy of FBLA-PBL, Inc.

▶ Family, Career and Community Leaders of America (FCCLA)

Family, Career and Community
Leaders of America (FCCLA),
Inc.
1910 Association Drive
Reston, VA 20191-1584
703-476-4900
www.fcclainc.org

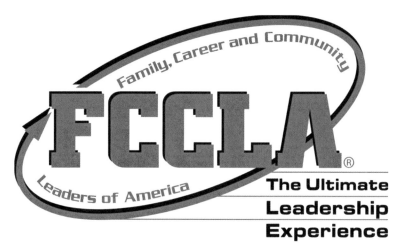

Figure 2-4. The official FCCLA emblem. Used by permission.

Family, Career and Community Leaders of America (FCCLA) is the national organization for students of Family and Consumer Sciences. The organization's mission is to promote personal growth and leadership development through Family and Consumer Sciences Education. Focusing on the multiple roles of family member, wage earner, and community leader, FCCLA members develop skills for life through character development, creative and critical thinking, interpersonal communication, practical knowledge, and career and technical preparation.

In 1943 the American Home Economics Association and the US Office of Education recommended development of a national organization for home economics students. This led to the development of Future Homemakers of America (FHA) in 1945. FHA merged with New Homemakers of America, an organization for African-American students, in 1965. When the Vocational Education Act of 1963 expanded home economics programs, FHA developed ways to meet the needs of students entering home economics for the first time. This led to the formation in 1971 of HERO chapters for occupational home economics students.

In 1999, delegates to FHA's National Leadership Meeting voted to change the organization's name to Family, Career and Community Leaders of America (FCCLA) to reflect its focus on career development, community service, leadership, and balancing families and careers.

The organization operates on national, state, regional and local levels, and offers two kinds of membership. *Active* members are students through grade 12 who participate in Family and Consumer Sciences Education. Chapters are represented nationally by ten members of the National Executive Council, selected by members at the National Leadership Meeting: these ten also serve on the National Board of Directors. Each state and local chapter chooses its officers through its own selection process.

Figure 2-5. FCCLA provides many opportunities for personal development and preparation for professional life. Photo courtesy of FCCLA, Inc.

▸ **DECA**

DECA
1908 Association Drive
Reston, VA 20191-1594
703-860-5000
www.deca.org

Figure 2-6. The official DECA Logo. Used by permission.

DECA is a national organization of more than 180,000 marketing students and 5,000 chapter advisors whose mission is to enhance the co-curricular education of students interested in entrepreneurship, marketing, and management. DECA seeks to help students develop skills and competence for marketing careers, build self-esteem, experience leadership, and practice community service. DECA advocates for marketing education and the growth of business and education partnerships.

DECA was founded in 1946 as the Distributors Club of America, and was endorsed that year by the National Association of State Directors of Vocational Education and the American Vocational Association. In 1950 the organization's name changed to Distributive Education Clubs of America. In 1962 a postsecondary division was created, changing its name in 1982 to Delta Epsilon Chi. In 1991, the full organization changed its name to the acronym DECA.

DECA operates and continually upgrades a system of competitive events in 36 different subject areas related to marketing, management, and entrepreneurship. Several events place members in problem-solving, role-play interaction with judges from the business community; others involve presenting judges with the results of written manuals. Event presentations are evaluated on specific, industry-validated performance indicators. Examples include online business simulations, Web design, and stock market investment strategies.

DECA identifies and serves five career clusters: Business, Management, and Administration; Hospitality and Tourism; Finance; Marketing, Sales, and Service; and Entrepreneurship.

The organization operates on international, regional, state, and local levels, with chapters in all fifty states, two Canadian provinces, Germany, Mexico, and Korea. DECA offers five levels of membership. The **High School Division** serves students enrolled in secondary marketing education programs. **Delta Epsilon Chi** members are college students preparing for careers in management, marketing, and related careers. The **collegiate** division enrolls education majors preparing to teach marketing and other related courses. The **professional** division consists of individuals who assist DECA members in career preparation; and the **alumni** division consists of former DECA and Delta Epsilon Chi members.

DECA also convenes two advisory boards, whose members serve by invitation. The National Advisory Board is comprised of more than 65 corporate and education leaders who help the organization award more than $250,000 in scholarship money. The Congressional Advisory Board is composed of members of Congress interested in marketing education.

Figure 2-7. DECA focuses on preparing students to become competent professionals in management and marketing careers. Photo courtesy of DECA Inc.

15

▸ **SkillsUSA**

SkillsUSA
PO Box 3000
Leesburg, VA 20177-0300
703-777-8810
www.skillsusa.org

Figure 2-8. The official SkillsUSA Logo. Used by permission.

SkillsUSA is a national organization serving more than 240,000 members (high school, college, and professional) who participate in technical, skilled, and service occupation training, including health occupations. The organization's mission is to help students develop employability, participation, and quality management skills that complement their occupational skills, as they strive to become world-class workers and responsible citizens.

SkillsUSA's activities build and reinforce self-confidence, work attitudes, and communications skills. The organization also promotes understanding of the free enterprise system and involvement in community service activities. SkillsUSA's programs include local, district, state, and national competitions in which students demonstrate occupational and leadership skills. Organizational programs also seek to establish industry standards for job skill training in the classroom.

High school teachers and students, seeking leadership training to complement their chosen vocations, founded the Vocational Industrial Clubs of America, Inc. (VICA) in 1965. A postsecondary division was added in 1969. VICA officially changed its name to SkillsUSA – VICA in 1999 ("SkillsUSA" was already in use as the name for the organization's competitive events). In 2004 the organization changed its name again, this time to SkillsUSA. The new name focuses attention on the vital importance of hands-on, academic, and employability skills for students.

SkillsUSA is comprised of the national association, state associations, and local chapters. Each local chapter elects a president, vice-president, secretary, treasurer, reporter, and parliamentarian. The organization offers six types of membership. ***Secondary division*** members are those enrolled in high school trade, industrial, technical and health occupations education. ***Postsecondary division*** members are those enrolled in a diploma- or certificate-earning major program or course sequence in preparation for education or employment in these fields. ***Direct*** members are students participating in authorized programs who do not have a state association to serve them. ***Professional*** members are recognized by state associations for their development efforts on behalf of student members. ***Alumni*** members are former active members. ***Honorary life*** members are recognized for significant contributions to SkillsUSA and related educational programs.

Figure 2-9. SkillsUSA members showcase their abilities in occupational skills events. Photo courtesy of SkillsUSA, Inc.

▶ **Technology Student Association**

Technology Student Association
1914 Association Drive
Reston, VA 20191-1540
703-860-9000
www.tsaweb.org

Figure 2-10. The official TSA Logo. Used by permission.

The Technology Student Association (TSA) is the national organization devoted to the needs of elementary, middle school, and high school students with an interest in technology. The organization's mission is to prepare its membership for the challenges of a dynamic world by promoting technological literacy, leadership, and problem solving skills, resulting in personal growth and opportunities.

TSA serves more than 200,000 students enrolled in technology education in grades K-12, most in middle and high schools. More than 2,500 technology education teachers serve as TSA advisors, using chapter activities to interest members and inspire them to pursue technology-based careers.

TSA began as the American Industrial Arts Student Organization (AIASA) in 1965, in affiliation with the Industrial Arts College Clubs (IACC). The two organizations parted ways in 1967, leaving AIASA as a separate organization for high school students. AIASA was recognized by the American Vocational Association in 1977 and by the US Office of Education in 1978. AIASA formally changed its name to the Technology Student Association in 1988 to reflect its commitment to the field of technology.

TSA is comprised of a national association, state associations, and local chapters. Student members participate in competitions, leadership training, and community service projects. Examples of competitions include website design, computer-aided design, flight endurance, and more than fifty others at middle and high school levels.

Each local chapter elects a president, vice-president, secretary, treasurer, reporter, and sergeant-at-arms. The organization offers five types of membership. *Active* members are students enrolled in technology education programs. *Associate* members are students enrolled in related fields. *Alumni* members are former active or associate members. *Professional* members promote TSA and technology education in education, business, and industry. *Honorary* and *Honorary Life* members are recognized by TSA's executive committee for their contributions to technology education.

Figure 2-11. TSA serves the needs of elementary, middle school, and high school students with an interest in technology. Photo courtesy of TSA.

▶ Business Professionals of America

Business Professionals of America
National Center
5454 Cleveland Avenue
Columbus, OH 43231-4021
800-334-2007
www.bpa.org

Figure 2-12. The official BPA Logo. Used by permission.

Business Professionals of America is a national organization for secondary, postsecondary, and middle level students enrolled in business and office education. The organization's mission is to contribute to the preparation of a world-class workforce through the advancement of leadership, citizenship, academic, and technological skills. Business Professionals of America helps its members develop leadership abilities, interest in the free-enterprise system, and competency in business and office occupations within the framework of career and technical education.

Business Professionals of America was formed in July 1966 as the Vocational Office Education Clubs of America, and one month later became the Office Education Association (OEA). Originally open to high-school students, OEA added an alumni division in 1971, a postsecondary division in 1975, and a middle level division in 2003. OEA's name was changed to Business Professionals of America in 1988 to reflect the changing goals of its members.

Business Professionals of America offers five divisions of membership. The *secondary* division includes members in high school business and office education courses. The *post-secondary* division includes members enrolled in business, office, or teacher education courses in colleges, universities, and proprietary schools. The *associate* division includes members in programs identified for special populations. The *middle level* division includes members enrolled in middle schools. The *alumni* division includes former active members from all divisions.

Within these divisions, the organization offers three classes of membership: *active* (those enrolled in courses or programs), *professional* (advisors and others involved in organizational development), and *alumni* (former active members). Each local chapter elects a president, vice-president, secretary, treasurer, historian, and parliamentarian.

Figure 2-13. Business professionals of America provides leadership development and builds competency in business and office occupations skills. Photo courtesy of Business Professionals of America.

▸ **Health Occupations Students of America (HOSA)**

Health Occupations Students of America, Inc.
6021 Morriss Road, Suite 111
Flower Mound, TX 75028
800-321-4672
www.hosa.org

Figure. 2-14. The official HOSA Logo. Used by permission.

Health Occupations Students of America (HOSA) is a national student organization for secondary, post-secondary, and collegiate students enrolled in health science technology. HOSA's mission is to enhance the delivery of compassionate, quality health care by providing opportunities for knowledge, skill, and leadership development of all health science technology education students, therefore helping students to meet the needs of the health care community.

In 1975, representatives from US states with student organizations focusing on health occupations met to plan a national leadership organization. Delegates from six states collaborated to form the American Health Occupations Education Student Organization (AHOESO). In 1976, delegates and advisors from these and several other states provided a formal structure for the new student organization: its name was changed to Health Occupations Students of America (HOSA).

HOSA's national organization is comprised of state associations that are made up of local chapters. Each local chapter elects a president, vice-president, secretary, treasurer, parliamentarian, reporter, historian, and chaplain. **Active** memberships are offered in a **secondary** division for high school students, a **post-secondary** division for students in full-time health science technology programs, and a **collegiate** division for students attending four-year institutions. An **alumni** division offers memberships for former active members. **Professional** members are those who participate in the development of health science technology programs, and **honorary** members are recognized for their significant contributions to the health care industry.

▶ **National Postsecondary Agricultural Student Organization (PAS)**

National Postsecondary Agricultural Student Organization (PAS)
6060 FFA Drive, PO Box 68960
Indianapolis, IN 46268-0960
317-802-4214
www.nationalpas.org

Figure 2-15. The official PAS Logo. Used by permission.

The National Postsecondary Agricultural Student Organization (PAS) is a national organization for students pursuing agriculture, agribusiness, and natural resources programs in approved postsecondary institutions. The organization's mission is to provide opportunities for individual growth, leadership, and career preparation.

PAS was first organized in 1979 and officially founded in 1980. Membership totals more than a thousand members from 56 chapters located in 18 states, and is available to students at institutions in all 50 states.

PAS is made up of national, regional, state, and local divisions. *Active* membership is available to any student enrolled in related programs in an institution offering bachelors or associate degrees, CTE diplomas, or certificates. *Associate* membership is available to anyone who provides support to the organization.

Figure 2-16. PAS provides growth, leadership, and career development opportunities for postsecondary agriculture students. Photo courtesy of the National PAS Organization.

► **National Young Farmer Educational Association (NYFEA)**

National Young Farmer Educational Association (NYFEA)
PO Box 20326
Montgomery, AL 36120
334-288-0097
www.nyfea.org

Figure. 2-17. Official NYFEA Emblem. Used by permission.

The National Young Farmer Educational Association (NYFEA) is the official adult student organization for agricultural education. The organization's mission is to promote the personal and professional growth of all people involved in agriculture. NYFEA strives to develop and provide educational, leadership, and civic opportunities to its membership and others. It provides a national framework to promote personal achievement, build business and environmental stewardship skills, and provide service opportunities for living and working in a local and global community. NYFEA was incorporated as an educational association for agriculture in 1982, and was recognized in 1990 as a CTSO by the US Department of Education.

NYFEA is organized nationally; delegates to the national organization represent individual state chapters. Participation is open to all interested individuals; emphasis is given to programs training young agricultural leaders, developing agribusiness skills, supporting children's education, and assisting with community development. NYFEA provides six membership levels: ***active***, ***contributor***, ***inactive***, ***corporate***, ***honorary***, and ***life***.

2. LESSON PLAN TO TEACH FUNDAMENTALS OF CTSO

The next step is to develop a plan to share this knowledge with students. While the optimal goal of the lesson plan is to secure all students' participation in the relevant CTSO, another realistic goal is to give them adequate information to choose whether to participate. Essential steps in creating a lesson plan include developing a list of *objectives*, identifying possible *interest approaches*, and identifying *resources* to develop the plan of instruction.

Clear *objectives* are essential to any lesson plan. Upon completion of the classroom unit, the student should be able to:

▸ Identify reasons for belonging to an organization in general, and why a member should attend a local chapter's meetings.
▸ Explain the CTSO being reviewed.
▸ List reasons for belonging to the CTSO.
▸ Distinguish why the CTSO specifically meets his or her needs.
▸ Identify major events in the history of the CTSO.
▸ Identify offices and areas of member responsibility in the local chapter.
▸ Identify the types of membership offered by the CTSO.

These are general objectives; more specific ones can be developed depending upon the nature of the specific CTSO. Addressing these objectives will ensure that the student is familiar with the CTSO being reviewed.

The next step is the *interest approach*: a plan to motivate the student to learn more about the CTSO. Successful approaches include, but are not limited to:

▸ Group discussions with former members who have become successful in later life, relating how membership in the CTSO helped develop their careers.
▸ Videos, slide shows, PowerPoint or other multimedia presentations depicting the CTSO and its activities.
▸ A chapter or club scrapbook that illustrates CTSO activities.
▸ An oral or written pre-test, covering facts about the CTSO.
▸ A display of trophies, plaques, and other awards won by CTSO members.

Each CTSO's website or official publications list reference booklets, pamphlets, videos, multimedia presentations, and other materials that will be useful in developing a lesson plan. Note too that experienced CTE education teachers are often overlooked as resources. In the authors' experience, CTE instructors are quite willing to share effective lesson plans with their peers.

Many states have developed lesson plans specific to their areas. The advisor should check the CTSO state office or the CTE education staff at a state university.

3. ORIENTING STUDENTS TO THE LOCAL CHAPTER

Students need to be oriented to the activities of the local chapter or club. Specifically, they should be aware that several activities will take place during class time, and others will extend beyond the classroom, shop, and laboratory. Two valuable resources for this purpose are the *program of activities (POA)* and the *chapter scrapbook*.

A valuable reference and orientation tool, the *POA* can be used for instruction and given to each student to follow throughout the school year. It should include:

- The local chapter's constitution and bylaws.
- A calendar and list of meeting dates and activities for the school year.
- Names of local and state officers.
- Names of committee members.
- The CTSO's creed, motto, and logo.

More information regarding the POA can be found in *Chapter 3: Developing Publishing and Implementing a Program of Activities (POA).*

The *chapter scrapbook* depicts organizational activities through photos, written descriptions, and news clippings; it can provide a visual depiction of the CTSO and make a different impact than a strictly verbal one. The scrapbook can be part of a formal classroom presentation by a chapter officer, providing an opportunity for questions and discussions, or can be placed in a location where students are able to review it at their convenience.

4. ENROLLING MEMBERS INTO THE CTSO

As stated above, the goal of the lesson plan is to secure full student participation in the relevant CTSO. Providing familiarity with the CTSO is a start, but it may also be necessary to inform students of membership benefits before officially enrolling them. *Benefits of membership* can vary between CTSOs, but the following are common to all:

- Participation in social and recreational activities.
- Opportunities to compete for awards.
- Travel opportunities.
- An expanded peer group.
- Public speaking experience.
- Opportunities to develop financial management, collaboration, and citizenship skills.
- National and state publications.

Figure 2-18. One of the benefits of belonging to a CTSO is the opportunity to travel. Photo courtesy of FCCLA, Inc.

An advanced or former member may be willing to list the benefits he or she received through membership; it may help to assign a dollar value to many of the benefits. In one example, a former CTSO member estimated that he received more than $900 worth of value from an investment of $12 for dues. He obtained this figure by assigning a dollar value to field trips, recreational activities, banquet meals, trips to conventions, and other events. Though the greatest benefits may not have a dollar value, such an illustration may encourage prospective members to join.

As with any organization, **enrollment** in a CTSO is not official until dues are paid. (Some CTSOs require dues to be paid by the school or institution; in these cases, all enrollees are automatically dues-paying members.) In most cases, three sets of dues are collected: one each for the national, state, and local organizations. Dues amounts for the national and state CTSOs are determined at a yearly convention and chapter dues by the local membership, usually at the first meeting of the year.

Many advisors find that a "package plan" is helpful for members. In this approach, the chapter pays all members' national and state dues out of its activity fund. Members later pay a combined dollar amount for local dues and reimbursement of the fund. Provisions should be made to assist members who cannot afford to pay dues. Many chapters provide an option for members to pay dues by earning money for the chapter. More information regarding dues payment can be found in *Chapter 8*: *Supervising the Financial Operation of the CTSO.*

CHAPTER 3
Developing, Publishing, and Implementing a Program of Activities (POA)

A CTSO provides challenging and coordinated activities for its members. As described in ***Chapter 2: Orienting Students to the Fundamentals and Principles of the CTSO***, a program of activities (POA) outlines major activities, sets specific goals, defines objectives for meeting those goals, and identifies the means for measuring progress.

While the basic responsibility for developing a POA lies with the student members, the advisor is responsible to supervise and assist in development and implementation. The development process provides the advisor with an opportunity to teach students about working together and in committees.

This section discusses the ***purpose of and need for*** the POA, and the sources needed for its ***development*** and ***implementation***. It presents the steps and deadlines to be used including practical guidelines for layout, printing, and distribution, and effective ways to evaluate past POAs.

Figure 3-1. Well-planned leadership activities are both challenging and fun. A program of activities should be the result of successful planning. Photo courtesy of the National FFA Organization.

Figure 3-2. A properly developed program of activities involves every member. Photo courtesy of DECA, Inc.

1. PURPOSE AND NEED

The POA is a written plan, developed and published annually, that specifies all activities a chapter seeks to accomplish during the school year. It includes a list of the CTSO's goals along with the objectives needed to achieve them. In some CTSOs, the POA is called a "program of work" or "yearly plan of activities". Much as a compass serves a traveler, the POA serves the chapter by pointing the way and guiding the membership toward activities that will best meet their personal and occupational needs. The POA may be divided into major divisions (e.g., student, chapter, community, and career) or into areas that correspond with the chapter's *standing committees*. Smaller chapters may prefer to use a few major divisions for the POA, and larger chapters may establish more.

A standing committee serves for the entire year, rather than for one specific purpose or event. Some CTSOs require the formation of committees that are determined on the national or state level, and others allow local chapters to determine committees. In either case, a local chapter may require additional committees beyond those recommended by higher offices. The most important point in developing the POA is to involve every member of the chapter. Some committees needed by a local chapter may include:

- ▶ Public relations committee
- ▶ Career skills committee
- ▶ Leadership committee
- ▶ Scholarship committee
- ▶ Human resources committee
- ▶ Finance committee
- ▶ Citizenship committee
- ▶ Support group committee
- ▶ Healthy lifestyle committee
- ▶ Recruitment committee

Each committee identifies goals for the chapter to accomplish, and various activities to help meet them. The POA enumerates these goals and activities, providing a sense of direction and greater likelihood of success.

Developing a POA is part of the leadership training that is essential in the educational process. By assuming duties and responsibilities for planned activities, members develop leadership, cooperation, and planning skills. The POA can also be an excellent public relations tool when the school and community are involved in the planning process, and can provide a means to evaluate and improve organizational activities year by year.

The advisor must guide students in selecting activities that are challenging, realistic, meaningful, and meet members' personal and career needs. To be effective, a POA should encompass the following qualities.

- ▶ *It should be challenging*: of interest to members, and one they will be motivated to follow.
- ▶ *It should develop leadership skills* for members, a major objective of a CTSO.
- ▶ *It should be educational,* consistent with the curriculum.
- ▶ *It should meet the needs of the majority of members*, balancing group goals with the needs of individuals.
- ▶ *It should stimulate, motivate, and develop member pride*.
- ▶ *It should develop employability skills,* complementing classroom and laboratory instruction with behaviors relevant in an occupational setting.

- *It should be consistent with organizational objectives* set by the national and state CTSO's own POAs.
- *It should be realistic:* easily accomplished within a set time frame, and within the chapter's budget.

The calendar year selected for the POA should match that of the state association's program calendar, although some adjustment may be required to accommodate the school year calendar. Planning should begin early enough to allow completion of the written plan within the first or second month. Many chapters start planning the upcoming year's activities during the previous year: a committee meets during the summer months to identify work areas, committee members, and activities. While the POA needs to be developed and approved by all members, this early start can set the stage for an organized year.

Note that many CTSOs require submittal of each chapter's POA to the state office by a specific date. Various awards are based upon this submission.

2. ASSISTING STUDENTS IN DEVELOPING THE POA

Developing a POA can be a simple task if each member knows his or her part of the process. The advisor needs to provide members with guidance on how to proceed and what is expected of them. While there is no single best method, many successful CTSOs follow these basic steps.

- ▶ *Select a group for overall responsibility:* A committee should be assigned to develop the POA. Members should determine a format, layout, and method of printing; assign specific areas of responsibility; gather information for each member's use; edit and coordinate the input of each member; and, ultimately, print and distribute the POA. While this committee is often comprised of chapter officers, the participation of other chapter members is always beneficial. As mentioned above, an early start for this committee provides a smooth transition.

- ▶ *Establish standing committees:* As mentioned above, standing committees serve the chapter for the entire year to fill particular need areas. Often, but not always, these need areas are assigned by the national or state CTSO. These committees should be given specific areas of the POA for which they will be responsible, and should cover all of the chapter's major activities. Each standing committee should be staffed with chapter members by assignment from the POA committee, taking each member's interests and preferences into consideration. The advisor should ensure that each member is given a job and serves on at least one committee. Since class time can be spent on CTSO activities, it may be helpful for all members of a committee to share the same class period.

- ▶ *Plan the activities:* It is always helpful for each standing committee to review the previous year's POA, retaining activities that are meaningful and effective, and eliminating those that were unsuccessful. It may also be instructive to review the national and state POAs, and those of other chapters.

- ▶ *Report the recommendations:* The chapter should devote one meeting to presentations from each standing committee regarding their particular recommendations. This allows all members to provide input, and to address activities and needs that may have been overlooked. Review drafts of committee recommendations can be distributed in advance. Recommendations can then be revised with this new input, and submitted to the POA committee for final editing.

- ▶ *Check with school authorities:* A list of activities should be given to the school administrator in charge of student activities. Administrative approval ensures that activities are appropriate for the school and makes it easier for the chapter to implement the POA as the school year proceeds.

Element	Description	Example	Comments
Program area	A standing committee should address each program area; in this example, scholarship.	"*Program area*: Scholarship."	The program area sets the tone for the rest of the steps.
Program goal	This should be the major goal that the committee believes the chapter should accomplish.	"*Program goal:* Each member will be recognized for improvement in scholarship, and will participate in scholarship improvement activities sponsored by the chapter."	There should be a major goal for each program area.
Objective	This should be a specific outcome that will demonstrate that the chapter has met the specific program goal. Several may be listed for each program area.	"*Objective:* By the end of the school year, at least 50% of chapter members will show an increase in overall grade point average (GPA) by at least two-tenths (0.2) of a point."	Note that the goal and out-come are written in a way that allows the committee and other observers to determine whether it has been met.
Activity	The "heart" of the POA, this is the method the chapter plans to use to accomplish each program goal. Several activities are usually listed for each goal.	"*Activity:* At the annual banquet in May, award a scholarship trophy to the member who improves his or her GPA the most during the school year."	It is important to list a specific date for the activity, as this becomes part of the activity calendar.
Amount budgeted	Though in many cases there is no cost involved in an activity, the chapter will need a cost estimate in order to determine which activities to sponsor.	"*Amount budgeted:* $20.00 for purchase of trophy."	The amount budgeted should also be recorded on a separate sheet and presented to the chapter treasurer.

Figure 3-3: Main components of a POA.

A standard format should be developed and followed when writing the POA. Items addressed generally include what is going to be done, who will be involved, when the event will take place, how many will participate, and how much it will cost. **Figure 3-3** shows the main components of a POA.

It is assumed that standing committee members (whose names should be recorded in the POA) will be in charge of accomplishing the tasks they specify. If other members are taking this responsibility instead, that should be specified.

The POA represents a good deal of hard work and cooperation on the part of the membership. An attractively printed and bound publication that can be shown to others is a significant public relations boost. As soon as the format is determined, the POA committee should begin to plan the overall layout and design for the final printing: this is determined in large part by chapter finances and member skill. Beginning chapters, therefore, should stick to a smaller and simpler format.

A suggested layout for the POA would include these items:

1. Table of Contents
2. Why Belong to a CTSO?
3. Membership Roster
4. Committee Members and Chairpersons
5. Local District, State, and National Officers
6. School Administration, Board of Education, and Advisory Committee
7. Chapter History
8. Calendar of Activities for the Year
9. POA for the Year
10. Budget
11. Chapter Constitution and By-Laws
12. Photos, Emblems, and Other Images

A beginning chapter in its first year, for example, may choose to include items 3, 4, 8, 9, 10, and 11, expanding to additional items in accordance with experience and resources. The advisor should encourage input from the membership regarding the POA layout and format, utilizing the creativity and innovation of the entire group.

As with the layout, chapter finances will determine the number of copies that can be printed and distributed. A suggested distribution hierarchy would provide copies in this order:

1. Each chapter member
2. Archives for future committees' use
3. School administrators
4. Advisory committee members
5. School board members
6. Interested school faculty
7. Key community members

Many chapters utilize the services of word processing, desktop publishing, and print shop classes within their schools to produce the POA, either free or at reasonable cost. Photographs and other images require special attention, as does the creation of an attractive cover. The chapter will want to recognize these efforts in the publication and at the annual awards banquet. If the advisor is an instructor in these areas, he or she can make production of the POA a classroom exercise, thus integrating the CTSO into the curriculum. In any case, the POA is an important promotional tool for the chapter and CTSO, and care must be taken in its duplication and distribution. Chapters may also find it valuable to include some parts of the POA on a chapter web site.

3. ASSISTING STUDENTS IN IMPLEMENTING THE POA

Even the best POA is of little value if it is not put into operation. The following suggestions will help the advisor lead his or her students through a successful implementation.

As described above, a calendar of activities is a month-by-month listing of events planned by each of the standing committees. An example is shown in Figure 3-4. The calendar should include organizational landmarks (e.g., dates to elect delegates) as well as chapter and state meetings. Some chapters include space

```
┌─────────────────────────────────────────────────────────────────┐
│                   CALENDAR OF ACTIVITIES                          │
│                        20XX/20XX                                  │
│                                                                   │
│  SEPTEMBER                                                        │
│  Executive Committee Meeting ...............................Sept. 1   │
│  Chapter Meeting ...........................................Sept. 12  │
│  District Leadership Contests ..............................Sept. 15  │
│  Blood Drive ...............................................Sept. 19  │
│  Mail State and National Dues ..............................Sept. 25  │
│  Publish Program of Activities .............................Sept. 27  │
│                                                                   │
│  OCTOBER                                                          │
│  Executive Committee Meeting ...............................Oct. 4    │
│  Chapter Meeting ...........................................Oct. 6    │
│  Program of Activities Due to State Office. ................Oct. 17   │
│  Select Delegates to National Convention ...................Oct. 22   │
│  Articles Due State Magazine ...............................Oct. 26   │
│  Begin Magazine Sales.......................................Oct. 28   │
│                                                                   │
│  NOVEMBER                                                         │
│  Executive Committee Meeting ...............................Nov. 5    │
│  Chapter Meeting............................................Nov. 8    │
│  Toys for Tots Campaign.....................................Nov. 12   │
│  KAFE Radio Program ........................................Nov. 16   │
│  State Public Speaking Contest .............................Nov. 18   │
│  Confirm Speaker for Chapter Banquet .......................Nov. 28   │
│  Order Supplies for Banquet ................................Nov. 28   │
│  End Magazine Sales.........................................Nov. 29   │
└─────────────────────────────────────────────────────────────────┘
```

on the calendar for a brief note evaluating each event. Extra space can also be provided for the addition of activities not included in the original plan. A copy of the calendar should be included in the POA and posted in all classrooms.

Each member should have his or her own copy of the POA, not only to become aware of activities, but also to identify his or her duties to the chapter. If possible, members should be able to serve on the standing committees of their choice, though experience and skill should play a factor in assignments. As stated above, the advisor should ensure that each member serves on at least one committee; this provides the member with an opportunity to give input and accept responsibility.

Standing committees should report at each chapter meeting. Committee members should recognize that they have dual responsibilities: coordinating their own organizational activities, and keeping the rest of the chapter informed. As stated above, it may be helpful for all members of a committee to share the same class period.

Note that the advisor is expected to provide guidance and encouragement; the members should run the chapter. Each member takes pride when he or she has a part in the chapter's coordinated operations.

CHAPTER 4
Electing and Training Chapter Officers

Capable and enthusiastic officers are essential to a chapter's success. The advisor must ensure that qualified officers are elected in a democratic manner. In this section the advisor will learn how to oversee the elections process, and to provide leadership training and assistance for the elected officers.

Figure 4-1. Installation ceremonies help ensure that officers begin their terms of office with a sense of pride and importance. Photo courtesy of FCCLA, Inc.

1. DUTIES AND RESPONSIBILITIES

Most chapters operate under the guidelines of a national and state constitution, set of bylaws, or both; in addition, each chapter has its own constitution, bylaws, or both. (The term "constitution" will be used to refer to a chapter' constitution, set of bylaws, or both.) A section of each document relates to officers: the advisor should ensure that the chapter's constitution does not conflict with either the national or state CTSO's constitution regarding the slate of officers or the procedures for their election.

Several officer positions are common to most CTSOs: *president*, *vice-president*, *secretary*, *treasurer*, *reporter* or *historian* (or both), *sergeant-at-arms* or *sentinel*, and *parliamentarian*. Titles may vary, so the advisor should check the relevant constitutions to determine the specific title of each office. National constitutions are usually found in each CTSO's student manual, handbook, or website; state constitutions are usually available from each CTSO's state office or website.

Additional officers may be added to meet a chapter's needs. This also provides more leadership opportunities for chapter members. Examples may include additional vice-presidents, a chaplain, a recreation leader, or a student advisor. Some chapters also elect a junior slate of officers, or a slate of officers representing each class: this provides leadership development opportunities in smaller groups, enables less experienced members to gain leadership skills, and helps teachers organize activities on a class-by-class level.

Figure 4-2. Local officers can learn the importance of ceremonies by observing state and national officers. Photo courtesy of the National PAS.

All officers are expected to exhibit leadership skills, including proficiency in conducting official ceremonies, parliamentary procedure, and public speaking. Officers must accept responsibility and lead by example. Each office has specific duties and responsibilities:each member should be familiar with these before elections are held. The major duties and responsibilities for each of the seven officer positions common to most CTSOs are summarized below; a more complete listing is provided in the Appendix. In addition, each CTSO's handbook or manual lists duties and responsibilities specific to each student group.

▶ The ***president's*** responsibilities involve coordination and leadership. As both a director and a manager, his or her main role is to see that the chapter meets its goals, both currently and in future years. Specific duties include presiding over and conducting meetings; representing the chapter at special functions and events; and keeping the chapter moving forward in a focused manner.

▶ The ***vice-president's*** responsibilities are to assist the president whenever required, be ready to take over for the president when necessary, see that all committees function properly, and provide other assistance when needed. He or she is also responsible for collecting committee reporting forms, and forwarding copies of these to the secretary.

▶ The ***secretary*** is responsible for an accurate accounting of all information needed by the chapter, and should be aware of all chapter and committee actions. Specific duties include preparing and reading the minutes of all meetings; providing the president with the agenda of all meeting business; preparing official correspondence; keeping accurate reports for national and state CTSOs; maintaining accurate chapter membership rolls; and counting and recording all votes.

▶ The ***treasurer*** is responsible for handling money and keeping accurate financial records for the chapter. Specific duties include keeping accurate records of all receipts and expenditures; preparing chapter budgets; following school financial procedures for transmittal of funds; and reporting on all expenditures at each meeting.

▶ The *reporter* or *historian* (some chapters have both) is responsible for the chapter's outreach efforts by developing community understanding and interest. Specific duties include maintaining the chapter scrapbook; preparing news articles and photographs to submit to local newspapers and broadcast stations regarding organizational events; and taking photos of events during the year.

▶ The *sentinel* or *sergeant-at-arms* is responsible for organizing and maintaining the meeting environment. He or she must be skilled at interpersonal interaction, and be able to handle details efficiently. Specific duties include setting up the meeting room; taking care of all chapter equipment and regalia; welcoming friends of the chapter; and arranging for refreshments and entertainment.

▶ The *parliamentarian* is responsible to ensure that meetings are organized and run in an equitable manner, usually in accordance with a resource such as *Roberts' Rules of Order*. Specific duties include working closely with the sentinel or sergeant-at-arms and other officers to ensure smooth coordination of meetings; answering questions about *Robert's Rules*; and ensuring both that the will of the majority is carried out and the rights of the minority are preserved.

Each officer is also expected to be familiar with the local constitution and POA; to spend extra time on committee meetings and other organizational activities, including encouraging members to participate; and generally to provide the needed leadership to plan and complete the chapter's activities.

Students should be informed about the duties of office, and any special requirements the advisor may expect. Handouts listing the duties and responsibilities of chapter officers can be distributed and discussed in class. Past officers, or a state or district officer, can be asked to address a class about what is expected of an officer.

2. ASSISTING STUDENTS TO SELECT QUALIFIED OFFICERS

While there is no one best way to elect officers, it should be noted that a student's experience with electing organizational officers can influence how he or she views the electoral process in other aspects of life. Thus it is important for members to be familiar with the democratic process of elections.

A *nominating committee,* selected by the executive committee and advisor, can help ensure that candidates are well suited for office. The committee can be comprised of final-year members (not

Figure 4-3. Election campaigns that are well organized and coordinated indicate that the advisor has helped prepare the members for office. Photo courtesy of FBLA-PBL, Inc.

eligible for the following year's offices) and other individuals who do not choose to run for office. The advisor should sit in on all nominating committee meetings. Nominating committee members should be informed of these guidelines:

▸ Each interview should be courteous, dignified, businesslike, and to the point. It is designed to acquaint the committee with the applicant, and to help determine who is best qualified to serve the organization. Leadership ability, appearance, speaking skill, reading ability, interest, enthusiasm, scholarship, occupational experience, attitude, habits, and conduct are all important points to consider.

▸ A careful job during the first interview will minimize the need to invite applicants back a second or third time.

▸ Personal friendship, favoritism, loyalty to the organization, and outside influence should have no part in the selection process. Even so, each committee member has an obligation to inform the others of all information he or she may know about an applicant.

▸ Interviews and discussions remain the business of the committee, and must not be passed along to others.

▸ Applicants should be observed during the interview process, both in and out of school.

▸ If an applicant demonstrates early in the interview that he or she is not a suitable candidate, the interview can be cut short.

Each candidate should be required to **submit a written application** for office. An example is provided in **Figure 4-4**. The nominating committee is responsible to print and distribute the applications to all interested members, and to set an adequate time frame for return of all completed applications. Completion of the application is a way to gauge the interest of potential candidates, and allows the nominating committee adequate time to schedule interviews. An officer interview form is provided in **Figure 4-5**.

The nominating committee should **present at least two candidates for each office**. In addition to candidates recommended by the committee, allow for nominations from the floor (provided they have completed an application for office). This allows a member who is defeated in a quest for one office to run for another.

It is essential that officers be elected by **secret ballot**. The advisor should ensure that this privilege is provided to all members. **Majority vote** should be required for election; this may require a run-off if three or more individuals are nominated for an office. Key steps for electing chapter officers include these:

▸ All members are informed of the various duties and responsibilities for each chapter office.
▸ Members establish and utilize a nominating committee.
▸ Members develop and use an application for each office.
▸ Members understand the importance of secret ballots.
▸ The advisor supervises the election of officers.
▸ The nominating committee advances the names of at least two candidates for each office, and additional nominations are accepted from the floor.

Application for Office of _____

Name _____ Age _____ Class _____

Student Organization Leadership Activities:

Leadership and Participation in School and Other Activities:

Are you willing to accept another office? ☐ Yes ☐ No
If so, which? (In order of preference)

What have you done to improve the organization?

What do you feel you can do to improve the organization?

Grade point average for current school year:_____
Grade point average for student organization related classes:
(by years) _____, _____, _____

Why are you running for an office?

Number of meetings attended since last June 1st:

Are you willing to spend extra time on Parliamentary Procedure?

Are you willing to spend extra time in planning and conducting meetings and activities?

APPROVAL OF PARENT OR GUARDIAN

_____ has our complete approval and our encouragement in his/her
quest for a chapter office, and we fully realize the additional time and work required of an office of the
organization if hc/shc is to fulfill his/her responsibilities properly.

_____
Parent's/Guardian's Signature

Figure 4-4. Chapter Officer Application

Officer Interview Form

1. Name_____

   Age _____ Year in School _____ Rank in Class _____

2. Student Organization Leadership Activities:

   Leadership Activities other than those of the Student Organization:

3. Occupation for which you are preparing:

   Are you employed?   ☐ Yes ☐ No If yes, where? _____

   What public speaking experience have you had?

   Describe how your present employment relates to your occupational objective.

4. Who are the people in this room, where are they from and what position do they hold?

5. Why do you want to be an officer?

6. What office are you interested in?

7. Give a description of your view of the responsibilities of the office for which you are applying.

8. What level of leadership training have you participated in on the:

   a) local level?

   b) state level?

   c) other?

9. Has candidate read a previously selected passage. How did candidate do?

10. What are your plans for the future?

11. Have you served as a member of a parliamentary procedure team?

    Level of participation _____
    (local, federal, area or state)

___APPEARANCE   ___PERSONALITY   ___JUDGEMENT   ___ENTHUSIASM   ___OVERALL

Figure 4-5. Chapter officer application.

3. INSTALLING NEW OFFICERS

An official *installation ceremony* should be convened to induct newly elected officers. The national or state CTSO should be able to help a local chapter select an appropriate ceremony. An installation ceremony allows new officers to indicate their willingness to perform their duties; increases other members' knowledge about the requirements of office; and instills pride and a sense of accomplishment in new officers.

Many chapters install their officers at the close of the year, often at an annual awards banquet. Others choose to hold the ceremony during a regular chapter meeting or a school assembly. In any case, the ceremony should be carefully planned and conducted in a decorous manner. Statements must be memorized, rehearsed, and correctly delivered for installing each new officer.

4. LEADERSHIP TRAINING AND INSTRUCTION

The advisor should provide leadership training to newly installed officers on the chapter level. Note that this text defines *leadership* as the ability to guide or influence others to work toward a meaningful goal, helping each to develop his or her ability as a group member. A good leader:

▶   Fosters active participation by the chapter.
▶   Promotes group cooperation and a desire to "pull together".
▶   Obtains essential information for group use.
▶   Encourages participation by all members.
▶   Stimulates evaluative thinking.
▶   Welcomes all contributions or suggestions, even those that some may think irrelevant.
▶   Encourages differences, as well as agreement of opinions.
▶   Sees that all sides are considered on all issues.
▶   Encourages growth and goal progress of all members.
▶   Constantly charts and summarizes the group's progress.
▶   Conducts continuous self-evaluation; strives to achieve individual goals as well as those of the group.

The advisor should provide each officer with copies of the local constitution, POA, and the national CTSO's manual or handbook. In addition, it is important for each officer to have a basic understanding of the rules of parliamentary procedure; a training session should be devoted to this task.

Specific officers may require additional training. The secretary may need to learn the particular format for writing each meeting's minutes, and the treasurer may need to learn to use a treasurer's report book. Sample formats for each are provided in Figures 4-6 and 4-7.

A chapter needs funds to be successful. Yet sometimes advisors fail to acquaint themselves with financial policies and procedures. The advisor and the treasurer will need to discuss the procedures and school regulations pertaining to collection and distribution of funds.

The reporter should be trained on how to write press releases. It will also be helpful for the advisor and reporter to schedule an introductory meeting with local news media members, allowing the reporter to ask questions of the professionals about how to prepare and submit copy.

MINUTES

Minutes of a Regular Meeting of the
_____ Student Organization
_____, _____

May 15, 20XX

Call to Order   The meeting was called to order at 7:00 p.m. by the president, Susan Smith

Roll   Forty-six members were present

Minutes   The treasurer reported:

Balance on hand April 15, 20XX..	$_____
Dues Received, 6 members...	$_____
Receipts...	$_____
Disbursements:	
Refreshments, $_____	
Student Handbooks, $_____..	$_____
Balance on hand, May 15, 20XX...	$_____

Committee Reports   Shelly Jones, chairperson of the nominating committee, reported that a meeting of this committee has been scheduled for Thursday at 7:00 p.m. Paul Downs, chairman of the recreation committee, reported that a skiing trip would be held during December. Further arrangements are being made.

Program   Mr. Jones, State Senator presented a talk, with question and answer session on leadership in the State Legislature

Adjourn   The meeting adjourned at 8:30 p.m. Refreshments were served following adjournment.

_____

Signed: President (President signs after approval at next succeeding meeting.)

_____

Signed: Secretary

Figure 4-6. Minutes form.

TREASURER'S REPORT

Date_____

Balance on hand
at date of last report...$_____

Receipts:
      Dues...$_____
      Magazine.......................................$_____
          Total Receipts...$_____

Disbursements:
      State and National Dues.............................$_____
      Secretary & Treasurer's book.......................$_____
          Total Disbursements...$_____
          Present Balance...$_____

Signed:_____
Treasurer

Figure 4-7. Treasurer's report.

The advisor should also be aware of training opportunities at the district, state, or national level, both for the chapter officers and for him or herself. Gathering information and exchanging ideas will help the advisor and officers conduct and expand chapter activities, and will help build enthusiasm and pride in the CTSO. The advisor should develop a list of references (e.g., books, magazines, websites, and other publications) and update it each year. Some items will be added and others eliminated as the advisor determines what materials work best for each group of students. Refer to the "Top Fifty" in Appendix IV for sample references.

It is essential for each officer to be able to recite his or her part in the chapter's opening and closing ceremonies. The tone of the meeting depends in large part on the quality of the opening ceremony; practice sessions may be needed to allow officers to master these. The advisor must memorize the recitations so that he or she can assist the officers. A good ceremony quickly develops pride and confidence in the officers, which is carried through to the subsequent meeting.

Training local officers is a year-round task, not limited to the first month or two in office. The best training an advisor can provide is to allow officers to make their own decisions at executive committee meetings, speak in public, and participate in state and national activities. By the end of the year, the officers will be a group of well-qualified leaders who will make the advisor's job easier.

Figure 4-8. These National FFA officers received training and preparation at the local chapter level. Photo courtesy of the National FFA Organization.

CHAPTER 5
Preparing Members for Participation in Local, District, State, and National Activities

Participation in CTSO activities promotes enthusiasm and pride among members. A wise advisor recognizes the motivational force these functions provide, and how preparing members for them can become a valuable teaching tool.

1. DETERMINING APPROPRIATE ACTIVITIES

Beginning CTE teachers are often overwhelmed by the multitude of awards programs, competitive events, and other activities sponsored by CTSOs. The question arises: "How can the chapter make time to participate in all these activities?" The answer, simply, is that it cannot. Chapters and their members do not participate in every activity, nor should this be expected.

Just as CTE covers a wide variety of occupations and interests, CTSOs provide activities to meet a wide variety of member interests. Not all are appropriate for each local setting. The advisor must take the total education program into account before helping members select activities for participation, and may choose to focus on successfully preparing for a few activities. Several factors should be considered:

▸ Member interests, needs, and occupational goals.
▸ How well an activity fits into the instructional program.
▸ Types of facilities and teaching materials required.
▸ Major goals of the local chapter.

Many CTSOs use contests to test specific member skills in a particular area: a competitive event in leadership, for example, may include skill contests in public speaking and parliamentary procedure. The advisor should review contest rules before preparing members for competition, as knowledge of the rules by the advisor and students is necessary for participation in competitive events.

Figure 5-1. Testing an occupational skill is always an appropriate activity for student participation. This student is testing his knowledge of plants at the National FFA Convention. Photo courtesy of the National FFA Organization.

Many chapters also sponsor their own local contests for member participation. Each should serve a specific purpose that is clearly understood by all, and should directly benefit members. The advisor and chapter should review local contests and activities annually to determine whether they continue to meet member needs and chapter goals.

Participation is a key determinant for whether to sponsor an activity. CTSOs emphasize both individual and group achievement. Some activities, therefore, are designed for individual participation, some for small teams, and others for the entire chapter. Generally speaking, an activity that provides a greater number of participation opportunities for members is best for the chapter.

Beginning advisors frequently find themselves conducting a hastily planned and organized activity. Unfortunately, these may discourage member participation. The advisor will learn to distinguish between small mistakes and major dilemmas, and may determine that resolution of minor problems may provide a learning experience for members. Even so, it is wise to list chapter activities on the calendar as early as possible.

Figure 5-2. Leadership activities which promote public speaking are important components of most CTSO's. Photo courtesy of National PAS Organization.

CTSOs develop leadership and personal skills, and so should the chapter's activities. Since no chapter can conduct every activity, the selection of activities should reflect the type of program taught, member needs and interests, occupational objectives, available time and resources, and chapter goals and objectives. All these elements should be included in the chapter's POA.

2. DEVELOPING A PROCESS TO PREPARE STUDENTS FOR ACTIVITIES

Effective participation in an activity or competition requires careful preparation. The advisor should schedule class time to prepare members for these activities.

Figure 5-3. Adults in the community can assist advisors in preparing students for participation in events and activities. Photo courtesy of Business Professionals of America.

Many beginning advisors find they need assistance with preparation. Official rules publications, manuals, and other publications from state and national CTSOs often contain checklists to help students and advisors. Experienced teachers, advisors, and alumni members may also be willing to offer advice and information. Programs from past competitions often provide ideas about preparing for specific events.

The preparation process can be broken down into four steps:

▸ First, members are ***made aware of available activities*** and skills required for participation.

▸ Next, the advisor helps members ***identify individual goals*** for specific activities, taking into account each member's abilities, interests, needs, and resources.

▸ Third, the advisor helps members ***refer to chapter goals***, usually within a committee structure, to determine whether to enter group competitions

▸ After the activity the advisor helps successful members ***set goals for further development***, and also assists ***those who fail to attain their goals***. Both require assistance with setting new goals and striving for further development. Those eliminated in competition may need special attention: they may need help accepting defeat with good grace, examining their goals, and determining how to make improvements or pursue alternative goals.

Note that while the advisor provides counsel and guidance, members make the ultimate decision about whether to participate.

It is important to maintain cumulative records of member participation for easy reference by the advisor and members, and for evaluation by the state CTSO.

3. DEVELOPING A PROCEDURE FOR SELECTING PARTICIPANTS

As mentioned above, an important role for the advisor is to inform members about available activities. An instructional unit on this topic is an easy way to ensure all students are informed about these opportunities: it should include brief descriptions and participation requirements for each available activity. Advance notice of upcoming activities is essential to encourage member participation.

Figure 5-4a & 5-4b. Activities are an important part of the educational experience. They should vary to match the technical and personal development skills taught in the instructional program. Photos courtesy of FCCLA, Inc. and SkillsUSA, Inc.

Written guidelines to determine which members will represent the chapter in each activity must be developed and understood by advisors and members alike. Criteria to determine award winners, team members, and individual contestants should be indicated clearly. The advisor must be able to explain to any member why he or she was either successful or unsuccessful in an activity.

Activities above the chapter level may limit participation (e.g., they may be limited to those who win at a district, area, or state level). CTSOs may allow only a small number of local members to attend conventions, and local chapters may have other limitations that restrict attendance (e.g., budget, school regulations, or transportation). Still other activities may be open and available to every member. As mentioned above, the advisor should encourage as many members as possible to participate in each activity: ample advance notice and planning time are therefore essential.

Figure 5-5. Teamwork and cooperation are as important as technical skills, and should be emphasized equally. Photo courtesy of DECA, Inc.

Figure 5-6. Competition can be stressful. Part of the advisor's responsibility is to encourage and support members who do not win. Photo courtesy of the National FFA Association.

Having written criteria for selection help members understand the requirements for participation in an activity, and allows them to strive to meet them. Competition scorecards, application forms, and other information used to select the winners should be available to all members: these explain why a member was successful or unsuccessful in an activity.

Examples include:

▶ Scoring students on skills competition activities, and using progress charts to choose representatives.

▶ Choosing outstanding first-year and senior members to represent the chapter.

▶ Requiring interested members to complete written applications that will be reviewed by a selection committee.

Note that members develop the criteria, and the advisor makes recommendations and ensures that applicable rules are followed. Members are more likely to accept the selection process if they participated in its development, and will question the procedure if they do not believe they had a stake in it.

4. ESTABLISHING PERFORMANCE STANDARDS AND GUIDELINES

Advisors must establish appropriate standards and guidelines for member and chapter participation, to ensure that the events are productive and meaningful. These should include scholastic requirements, rules concerning member conduct, and consequences of rule violation. Guidelines should be clearly written and distributed to each member.

Chapter members should develop the standards and guidelines under the advisor's guidance. School regulations should be reviewed and incorporated, and approval obtained from school administrators. The advisor should remember that, while the chapter develops and approves the standards, it is his or her responsibility to enforce them. He or she should clearly explain what is expected of members, and the consequences to be expected if standards are not met.

Many schools require *parental approval* for participation in an event. A sample approval form is shown in Figure 5-11. Similarly, some national and state CTSOs provide forms that address member *supervision*, personal *liability*, and *medical information*. Examples are provided in Figure 5-13 and Figure 5-10; these can be used as guidelines if the local chapter chooses to develop its own forms.

If the activity requires absence from school, students should be informed of procedures for *making up missed work* (e.g., obtaining and completing assignments ahead of time).

Figure 5-7. Good selection criteria are necessary to ensure the chapter/club is well represented at state and national events. Photo courtesy of SkillsUSA, Inc.

After standards and guidelines have been developed, the advisor needs to develop a plan to enforce them. These suggestions may prove helpful.

▸ Students who are difficult to supervise during regular class periods often create problems on extended trips. Yet it is hard to defend exclusion of members based on how they *might* behave! One solution is to inform members that a period of appropriate, non-disruptive behavior is a prerequisite for participation. Many advisors assume that members will be motivated to behave well at an activity simply by the reward of "being there". Experience shows that when attendance is earned by meeting established criteria, members recognize the privilege involved and respect the rules that govern participation.

▸ Housing must be carefully planned in advance. Room assignments must be made judiciously: overcrowding and inattentive roommate pairings will often result in disruption. Experienced advisors know that agreeable accommodations result in better behavior. A sample housing form is provided in Figure 5-12.

▸ Meals can be better provided for large groups in cafeteria-type restaurants than in smaller establishments. Calling ahead to reserve space allows restaurant staff to better accommodate a group.

▸ Members that are kept busy usually create less disruption. Many events allow for some free time: the wise advisor will schedule activities during this time period (e.g., tours, recreation, study sessions, or supervised free time). It is a good idea to confirm member attendance at all scheduled events.

▸ Unsupervised members in hotel or motel areas are the biggest source of trouble during CTSO activities. Even the "best" members can create problems if supervision is not provided. Proper planning minimizes this problem. Additional advisors may be needed with larger groups.

Preparing and supervising members at CTSO activities can be an enjoyable and fulfilling experience with attentive planning and supervision. A checklist for use in preparing members for CTSO activities is provided in Figure 5-9.

Figure 5-8. Standards and guidelines should be developed to help students exhibit mature behavior when participating in CTSO activities. Photo courtesy of DECA, Inc.

Checklist for Preparing Members for
Student Organization Activities

☐   1. All possible awards programs, contests, and activities have been reviewed for possible participation.

☐   2. The chapter or club and all members have received assistance in selecting appropriate activities.

☐   3. The instructional program includes covering preparation for student organization activities.

☐   4. Written procedures have been established and approved by students and school administrators for selecting members for participation in various activities.

☐   5. Activities scheduled have been placed on the official school calendar well in advance of the scheduled date.

☐   6. Students have received assistance in identifying individual goals for specific activities and functions.

☐   7. Students have identified goals for chapter or club participation in student organization activities and included these in the annual program of work.

☐   8. Written standards have been developed and approved by students for participation in student organization activities.

☐   9. Written standards have been approved by school administrators and are in accord with school regulations and policies.

☐   10. All students have been informed of the standards and guidelines for participation in student organization activities.

☐   11. Standards are consistently maintained and enforced by the student organization advisor.

Figure 5-9. Checklist for Preparing Members for Student Organization Activities

MEDICAL INFORMATION

Student _____   Parent/Guardian _____
Spouse (if married) _____   Address _____
Home Address _____   Phone: Work_____ Home_____
Phone: Work_____ Home_____
Student's Doctor _____   Alternate Contact _____
Address_____   Address _____
Phone: Work_____ Home_____   Phone: Work _____ Home _____

Please describe completely and medical conditions (past or present) being treated which may reoccur or be a factor in medical treatment (include allergies, medicine reactions, disease of any kind, physical handicaps, heart or lungs problems, seizures, convulsions, blackouts, etc.) If currently taking medications, state the medication and prescribing physician and phone number:

_____
_____
_____

We certify that the information that the information described above is accurate and complete to the best of our knowledge. We understand that each individual is responsible for their own insurance coverage during this meeting or conference.

Name of Company_____   Policy No. _____

NOTARY

Instructions: Parent/Guardian: Please check and sign ONE of the statements below.

☐ I give permission for immediate medical treatment (as required) by the attending physician.

*_____ is the person authorized to grant permission for medical treatment for my son/daughter.

Parent/Guardian Signature_____ Date_____

☐ I **DO NOT GIVE** permission for medical treatment until I have been contacted.

If, after I have been contacted, I consent to medical treatment, *_____ is the person authorized to grant permission for medical treatment for my son/daughter.

Parent/Guardian Signature_____ Date_____
*Name of teacher or sponsor

State of _____   County of _____

Acknowledged before me this _____ day of _____,_____
My commission expires:_____ _____   _____
                                                  Notary Public

Figure 5-10. Sample medical information forms.

APPROVAL FORM

Name of Student _____ Age _____

School _____ School Phone _____

Conference _____ City (State) _____

Dates _____

SIGNATURES

Instructions: This form must be completed for each student attending a Career and Technical Education Student Conference. Signatures acknowledge that all parties have read and concur with the information contained herein. Information concerning sponsor delegation shall be completed prior to affixing of signatures. **Parents of minors mst also sign the medical form.**

School Official	Title	Date	Chapter Advisor	Date

Parent/Guardian	Date	Student	Date

SPONSOR DELEGATION

_____ School designates the adult(s) listed as the sponsor(s) who will supervise students during the State or National Conference.

Chapter Advisor _____

Other Adult Sponsors _____

_____

_____

Special Instructions: This section must be completed by an official of the school that agrees to sponsor students from another school.

The sponsors (listed above) from _____ school agree to sponsor students from_____ school during the State or National Conference. Our school is in complete agreement with this arrangement.

School Official	Title	Date

Figure 5-11. Sample approval form.

HOUSING FORM

Print or Type All Information

School _____   Advisor _____

Address _____   Phone _____

Date of Arrival _____   Time of Arrival _____

Date of Departure _____   Arriving by: ☐ Bus   ☐ Car   ☐ Van

Method of Payment: ☐ Cash   ☐ Check   ☐ Purchase Order   ☐ Credit Card

Instructions: 1. Print or TYPE names of ALL persons occupying each room
                  2. Use "M" for Male and "F" for Female
                  3. Select type of room desired
                  4. Supplemental list for additional rooms MUST use same format (can make copy of page)

NAME(S) (last name first)   **M/F**   **ACCOMMODATION**

Room No. 1. _____   **CHECK ONE:**

            2. _____   Single ☐   Trip ☐

            3. _____   Twin   ☐   Quad ☐

            4. _____

Room No. 1. _____   **CHECK ONE:**

            2. _____   Single ☐   Trip ☐

            3. _____   Twin   ☐   Quad ☐

            4. _____

Room No. 1. _____   **CHECK ONE:**

            2. _____   Single ☐   Trip ☐

            3. _____   Twin   ☐   Quad ☐

            4. _____

NOTE: Please re-check all items for correct information

Figure 5-12. Sample housing form.

Personal Liability Release

Instructions: Paragraph "A" applies to students of less than legal age in this state. Parents/Guardians of these students agree, by affixing their signatures to page one of this form, the conditions set forth here-in.

Paragraph "B" applies to all students and each agrees, by affixing his/her signature to page one of this form, to the conditions set forth here-in.

A

Being parents/guardians of a son/daughter who is a member of a Career and Technical Education Student Organization, we hereby agree to release the CTSO, its representatives, agents, servants, and employees from liability for any injury to said minor - resulting from any cause whatsoever occurring to said minor at any time while attending a conference or meeting of the CTSO including travel to and from said meeting, excepting only such injury or damage resulting from willful acts of such representatives, agents, servants, and employees.

B

As a member of a CTSO, I hereby agree to release the CTSO, its representatives, agents, servants, and employees from liability for any injury resulting for any injury resulting from any cause whatsoever, occurring at any time while attending a conference or meeting of the CTSO, including travel to and from said meetings or conferences, excepting only such injury or damage resulting from willful acts of such representatives, agents servants, and employees. Furthermore, having read and understood completely the delegate code, practices, and procedures which will govern the conduct of students attending said meetings or conferences, I hereby do agree to follow the procedures and practices as described. I fully understand that this is an educational activity and will, to the best of my ability, apply myself for the purposes of learning and uphold the finest qualities of a delegate representing this CTSO.

ACTION TO BE TAKEN WHEN STUDENTS VIOLATE DELEGATE CONDUCT GUIDELINES

Penalties for violation of the Delegate Conduct Guidelines will be determined by the severity of the violation. The following items are considered critical and may be acted on as indicated:

Critical Items: Numbers 3, 4, 5, 8, 11, 15 (see page 52)

Possible Action: The appropriate chapter advisor or sponsor will be notified of the violation and the following action(s) may be taken:
  A. Student(s) may be disqualified from participating in the conference/meeting and may forfeit any honors received..
  B. Students(s) may be sent home immediately, in which event the following procedures will be followed:

▸ Local school official and /or parents will be contacted.
▸ Reasonable care will be exercised to insure that the safest and most expedient means of transportation back to the state and/ or local school is used.
▸ The local school and/or parents/guardians will be responsible for meeting the student at a prearranged destination.
▸ The local school will be responsible for the appropriate action to be taken with the student involved upon return to school.
▸ Disciplinary action (other than above) may be taken in accordance with the severity of the violation. This action will be determined by the appropriate State Advisor and/or State Supervisor in consultation with the chapter advisor or sponsor of the student involved.

Figure 5-13. Sample personal liability form.

Delegate Conduct Guidelines

1. The term *delegate* shall mean any member attending a CTSO meeting or conference.

2. Delegates shall abide by all conference rules in a manner that will bring credit to their CTSO.

3. Delegates shall keep their adult advisors and/or sponsors informed of their activities and whereabouts at all times.

4. Delegates must stay in housing designated by their chapter advisor during the conference.

5. Delegates shall use authorized transportation only.

6. Dates and escorts shall be permitted to authorized activities only and in the company of official delegates only.

7. Delegates are permitted to attend authorized activities only.

8. No alcoholic beverages or illegal drugs shall be possessed or used by delegates at any time under any circumstances.

9. Delegates shall respect and abide by the authority delegated to the presiding officers, chapter advisors, sponsors, and state staff.

10. Delegates shall attend all general sessions and activities assigned, including workshops, competitive events, committee meetings, etc. for which they are pre-registered - unless engaged in some other authorized assignment taking place at the same time.

11. Curfew each night will be designated on the program, and all delegates will be in their rooms by curfew.

12. Dress regulations established for the conference/meeting functions shall be adhered to by all delegates.

13. Identification badges must be worn to all official functions and/or as directed.

14. Smoking will not be permitted.

15. Boys will not be in girls rooms and/or girls shall not be in boys rooms at any time - unless an adult sponsor is present.

16. Delegates violating or ignoring the above conduct guidelines - or those set forth by their respective national organization - subject their club's entire delegation to being unseated, it's candidates being disqualified, and any honors or offices being cancelled and withdrawn from members of their delegation.

Figure 5-14. Sample delegate conduct guidelines.

CHAPTER 6
Helping Members Advance Through the CTSO

Almost all CTSOs use various **degrees** of membership to recognize accomplishments and signify advancement in the group. In this section, the advisor will learn about the qualifications and requirements for degrees, and how to help members apply and qualify for them. Suggestions are also provided for developing and using application forms for local degree programs.

Note that degrees are generally used to denote a **level of active membership** and should not be confused with the **classes** of kinds of membership many CTSOs establish (e.g., active, alumni, honorary, associate, or professional).

It is generally understood that degrees at the local, state, and national levels become progressively more difficult to attain, and therefore that a smaller number of members achieve the more difficult or advanced degrees. Advanced degrees require participation in activities above the chapter level, along with completion of other criteria.

Degrees allow members an opportunity to develop and improve their skills. While not all CTSOs sponsor competitive activities, there is some element of competition in every CTSO. Individual members can be encouraged to take on a competitive approach for skill building, even if they may only be competing against themselves. Multi-level degree programs require development of short-range objectives to reach the immediate goal, and long-range plans to reach a more advanced degree. They allow members to:

▸ Achieve early in their membership by mastering easier tasks for lower-level degrees.

▸ Gain recognition during various stages of membership.

▸ Work toward goals that are realistic and match their skill level.

▸ Work with the advisor on developing skills and abilities.

▸ Establish educational, personal, and career goals.

Figure 6-1. Degree programs promote friendly competition. Photo courtesy of DECA Inc.

1. INFORMING MEMBERS OF DEGREE REQUIREMENTS

The optimal goal for an advisor is for each member to attain the highest degree possible, based on individual ability. To that end, it is imperative that the advisor has a thorough understanding of the requirements and qualifications for all available degrees, and conveys this information to the members.

Local chapters confer *local degrees*. Many CTSOs set minimum requirements for local degrees, allowing chapters to establish additional requirements. Generally, local degree requirements should be easily attainable by most members with information and guidance from the advisor.

There are many ways to communicate degree requirements to members. An earlier section suggested a classroom unit of instruction, which can utilize handouts and other means of communicating this information. Classroom discussions ensure that all members fully understand the requirements. Bulletin board displays, chapter meeting discussions, and one-to-one conversation with members are other ways to convey these factors.

While most degree-related information can be presented to a group of members, each individual member must develop a plan for attaining the degree. Some may need very little help, while others will need more. Records of member participation will be helpful for developing individual plans. The advisor is responsible to establish and maintain a member record system; completing and updating individual records is the member's responsibility. Many advisors use regular class time to complete and update member records.

Meeting the requirements for a local degree can give members a sense of accomplishment, and motivate them to set goals to progress further in the CTSO. This usually means pursuing *advanced degrees*, which are usually established at the national and state level. The advisor should carefully review CTSO publications and other information to develop and provide accurate lists of degree requirements, updating these annually.

Some advisors cover local and advanced degrees during the same instructional unit; others wait until the first degrees are attained by most members before discussing the advanced degrees. Either way, members should be informed that degree attainment requires a stepwise approach: each degree builds upon the previous one, and helps the member prepare for the next.

The objective of a CTSO is to help the member develop as an individual. The degree program is only one of many ways the CTSO accomplishes this. Teaching skills for personal development and degree attainment keeps interest high and maintains continuity of instruction. When the majority of members are ready to work toward their next degrees, the advisor can assist them by preparing all instructional units ahead of time.

2. APPLICATION FORMS FOR LOCAL DEGREES

The chapter can develop an application form for a local degree with the advisor's input. The use of application forms directly involves members in the process of reviewing applicants' qualifications.

Local degree applications should comply with all national and state degree requirements. Once these are met, the application should reflect the goals and objectives of the local chapter. Member input is necessary in developing the applications; this in turn requires members to understand the purpose and requirements of the local degree program.

As with the POA, applications should be professionally developed and distributed to all members. They must also be kept current to reflect the latest requirements. Some national and state offices have sample applications that local chapters can modify for their own needs. A sample is provided in **Figure 6-3**.

The advisor should review the application in class with all members, and then have each member complete an application to be kept in the student file. Class time should be allocated periodically to update these applications. A target date should be established for members to meet all degree requirements, well in advance of the date upon which degrees will be conferred. This allows the advisor and committee to review all applications, and provides sufficient time for students to complete the requirements.

Members are responsible for submitting applications prior to the deadline; all requirements for advanced degrees should be completed before submission. Requirements for local degrees may or may not be accepted after submission depending upon the philosophy of the chapter and advisor, but all should receive the same treatment (e.g., either all accepted or all rejected).

A fair and complete evaluation is essential to the degree program. An evaluation committee made up of members is a good way to judge applications, providing student leadership opportunities and making best use of the advisor's time. The committee members should be given complete instructions regarding the evaluation process. They should also clearly state their reasons for acceptance or rejection on the application. The advisor should review and approve all applications: the final responsibility for awarding the degrees rests with him or her, and the program can be damaged if undeserving members are rewarded or deserving members overlooked.

Figure 6-2. Committees provide a good means of evaluating degree applications.
Photo courtesy of Gary Farmer, University of Georgia.

Degree Application

Degree or Rank _____

Requirements: (check when completed)

* Club Knowledge
- [ ] 1. Know the motto
- [ ] 2. Know the colors and be able to give their meaning
- [ ] 3. Be able to give the six points of the creed and discuss them
- [ ] 4. Describe the Official Emblem and give its meaning
- [ ] 5. Know the purposes of the organization
- [ ] 6. Be able to recite the pledge
- [ ] 7. Know the official dress of the organization
- [ ] 8. Know and be able to discuss the organizational structure of the local club

* Leadership Skills
- [ ] 1. Know and understand the fundamental principles of American democracy
- [ ] 2. Possess minimum skills in parliamentary procedures
- [ ] 3. Be able to list the officers of your local club and discuss the duties of each

* School Knowledge
- [ ] 1. Know and understand the structure of your school
- [ ] 2. Know how your training program relates to the school system
- [ ] 3. Have an awareness of our teachers' duties and responsibilities
- [ ] 4. Know what your responsibilities are to your own education, to your fellow students, and to the school

* Service Requirements
- [ ] 1. Participation in club projects, activities, and general service to the local club
- [ ] 2. Regular attendance at club meetings
- [ ] 3. Regular voting at all business meeting for officers and various issues
- [ ] 4. Participation in school-wide service projects and activities
- [ ] 5. Participation in committee meetings

Date of Evaluation _____ **Time** _____ **Place** _____

Approved _____

(Signature of Committee Chairman)

Figure 6-3. Degree application.

3. QUALIFYING FOR ADVANCED DEGREES

Each member should establish his or her own goals for advancing within the available degrees. The advisor should provide members with applications encourage and assist members in setting goals that are both challenging and realistic, and establish timetables for meeting degree requirements.

Experience is the most important factor for advisors seeking to help members set goals. New advisors can ask older members to pair with younger ones to discuss goal setting, degrees, successes, and overcoming obstacles. State officers are also valuable resources, and may be willing to meet with members to discuss goals.

Experienced advisors know that members often become so involved with activities that long-range goals are forgotten: thus it is the advisor's responsibility to monitor members' progress and keep them "on task".

Keeping members engaged and proactive is a difficult task. Incentives and competition among students sometimes help to maintain motivation. For example, some advisors award a prize to the first member who completes a specific requirement or degree. Periodic review of applications during class time reorients members to the tasks, and helps encourage members to keep pace with one another.

Figure 6-4. Supporting evidence is equally as important as the application. Photocopies of awards and activities help document the written application. Photo courtesy of DECA,Inc.

Applications for advanced degrees should be completed completely and accurately. The advisor and selection committee have first-hand knowledge of the applicant for a local degree, but this personal connection is lost on the district, state, regional, and national level. The application and supporting documents are all that the degree reviewers have upon which to base their decisions.

These suggestions may be helpful:

▸ ***Avoid leaving blank spaces on the application.*** With limited space on the application form, assume that all the questions presented are important.

▸ ***Use answer spaces wisely***, avoiding duplication and unnecessary words. Each comment should directly address the question being asked.

▸ If the application requests photos, captions, or stories, ***submit the maximum amount permitted***.

▸ Stories about the applicant's accomplishment should ***be accurate, clearly written, and provide information that will advance the member's case***. Avoid repetition.

‣ *Neatness counts*. Overall appearance and uniformity throughout will help keep an application from being rejected out-of-hand. Applications should be typed, strikeovers should be avoided, and corrections should look clean. Retyping an application page can sometimes make the difference between acceptance and rejection. Applications prepared with a computer word processing program are usually preferred, as they are the easiest to complete and edit.

‣ *Display supplemental materials neatly and creatively*. Photos should be at least 5"x7" in size; electronic images must be submitted in the requested format. Only use those photos that advance the application.

‣ *Check all mathematical calculations.* Inaccuracies can cause an application to be rejected.

‣ *Spelling and grammar errors indicate carelessness.* Carefully check spelling and grammar. Remember that a computer "spell check" may not catch all errors.

‣ *The application must appear credible to the selection committee.* Document and explain any part of the application that may appear questionable.

‣ *All required parties should sign the application and submit it to the advisor for final review.* It should be mailed in enough time to reach its location by the deadline. The advisor should allow ample time for review; an adequate job cannot be done a few moments before the mailing deadline.

‣ *Online submissions and applications.* Many applications can be completed electronically; however, most advanced degree applications are still submitted in "hard copy". Not only do these provide original signatures, but many reviewers also prefer to use paper copies. Chapter advisors may choose to implement electronic applications at the local level.

4. <u>RECOGNITION</u>

Degrees of membership help motivate members toward personal accomplishment. To this end, recognition should be given to those who attain each degree. State and national offices provide part of the recognition for advanced degrees. Each member receiving a degree should receive recognition, including a certificate, pin, plaque or trophy, during an official degree ceremony.

The chapter officers and advisor should plan the degree recognition ceremonies. Dates should be selected well in advance and listed on the school and chapter activity calendars, allowing officers time to prepare, memorize, and rehearse speeches. Parents, teachers, and other guests may be invited. Guest speakers, if any, need to be notified in advance.

As with all meetings, the recognition ceremony should be well planned. The meeting room should have ample seating, and awards should be arranged to allow quick and easy presentation. Recognition ceremonies are excellent public relations tools, so the chapter secretary or reporter should notify local newspapers to cover the event and take photos. Members should dress appropriately, and all officers should be prepared to recite their parts in the ceremony. More information about award and recognition ceremonies can be found in *Chapter 9: Helping Members Develop and Conduct Award and Recognition Programs.*

A checklist covering the responsibilities for degree programs is provided in Figure 6-5. It is often assumed that good public relations will be an automatic by-product of a well-run CTSO. This, however, is not always the case. The community and the school may not always take note of the CTSO's good works, so a public relations program is needed to tell the story.

Degree Program Checklist

☐ All constitutional requirements for degrees were read and passed on to the members.

☐ Degree requirement lists were made and handed out to each member.

☐ Classroom time was scheduled on a regular basis for assisting students with degree applications.

☐ Every member developed plans for degree advancement

☐ A degree file was kept on every student.

☐ Every member maintained a degree application that was updated periodically.

☐ Every qualified student applied for an advanced degree.

☐ Chapter officers conducted formal ceremonies recognizing individuals who received local degrees.

☐ News articles were prepared to recognize individuals receiving degrees.

☐ Certificates, pins, or other appropriate recognition were presented to degree recipients during degree ceremonies.

Figure 6-5. Degree program checklist.

NOTES

CHAPTER 7
Supervising the Development and Conduct of a Public Relations Program

For any student organization to be a vital part of a community or school, it is necessary for the public to recognize what the organization does: a CTSO is no exception. In addition, almost every activity of a CTSO requires support from external individuals and groups. Everything a CTSO does contributes to its public image, thus it is important for the advisor to supervise the development and conduct of a public relations program.

A public relations program shows the community that the CTSO's activities and those of individual members are exceptional, and emphasizes the educational achievements of the CTSO and its participants. It also provides members with educational opportunities to develop skills in leadership, communications, and other areas.

The "public" in "public relations" refers to almost anyone or any person outside the CTSO. The more the public knows about a CTSO, the more likely they are to provide needed assistance: thus highly visible organizations best meet the needs of their members. Simply put, the purpose of a public relations program is to inform people about the CTSO. Citizens like to know that their tax dollars are being spent on worthwhile, educational activities. Community members appreciate knowing about students who are "doing something good". The school system benefits from public recognition of quality education, and a positive public image helps secure financial aid for trips, equipment, uniforms, and other organizational expenses.

A good public relations program encourages student participation. Too often, students may have insufficient or incorrect information about a CTSO. Effective public relations can help the CTSO reach students who may not otherwise belong. Individual members also benefit from good public relations: public recognition of accomplishments and activities creates happy, fulfilled members.

Figure 7-1. Photographs showing members involved in worthwhile activities contribute a great deal to the public's perception of a CTSO. Photo courtesy of FBLA-PBL, Inc.

A good public relations program brings at least two direct, tangible benefits to a CTSO and its members: *financial assistance* and *business participation*. Since donations often provide a major portion of a CTSO's funding, a public relations program helps by letting people know how their donations are spent. Many donors are more willing to contribute when they have an interest in the activities a CTSO undertakes.

Similarly, public relations programs inform potential employers about various job-training opportunities, and assist them in providing quality on-the-job training that promotes the business and aids the CTSO. A good public relations program will often increase the number of businesses willing to serve as job training sites.

1. CODE OF ETHICS AND CONDUCT

Each CTSO has a code of ethics or rules of conduct. These address such matters as dress code, respect for others, honesty in dealings, and pride in the CTSO; some also list rules specific to certain group activities. These documents can be an excellent aid to good public relations. Members of the public take note of the actions of CTSO members, and carry away a positive impression of the CTSO and its mission when rules of appropriate conduct are followed.

Each prospective member should be given a copy of the code or rules to help determine whether the CTSO meets his or her needs. Early in membership, the advisor should review and emphasize the importance of the code or rules. The information can be conveyed to members in an entertaining but informative way (e.g., playing a game that involves knowledge of the code, or creating posters or bulletin boards that represent the code in creative ways). The national office of the CTSO may have guidelines and resource material that can be used to instruct members in these matters, both in a group and individually.

Note that even the most comprehensive code of ethics or rules of conduct will not ensure a good public image unless members put them into action. Peer support and member pride in the CTSO are more effective for ensuring appropriate conduct than any number of lectures and reminders from an advisor.

2. DEVELOPING A POSITIVE PUBLIC IMAGE

Presenting a good public image begins with pride in belonging to the CTSO. The advisor must show pride in the CTSO and the accomplishments of the chapter. He or she should point out the service and educational benefits of each activity, and how they help each member. Talking about chapter accomplishments helps bolster the pride of the entire group.

Figure 7-2. An official emblem can be attractively displayed to promote interest in the CTSO. Photo courtesy of National FFA.

Part of the CTSO's mission is to help members develop self-confidence and project a positive image. It is often assumed that teenagers and young adults automatically know how to conduct themselves, dress and groom appropriately, and maintain their hygiene. It may seem self-evident that good grooming and hygiene lead to good public relations for the CTSO. However, all members will usually benefit from instruction in presenting a good image. Successful methods include role-playing exercises, checklists for member use, demonstration of proper methods for tying ties and scarves, and presentations from health care professionals.

The most visible clue to the public that a person is a member of a CTSO is his or her apparel. Similar clothing that is easily recognizable can be an inexpensive, effective way to promote the CTSO. Some CTSOs have specific rules for wearing identifying apparel such as blazers, jackets, and uniforms. The advisor should be aware of these standards and make them known to members, perhaps requiring them to sign an agreement before purchasing these items. In some cases, students may need reminders about how to wear official clothing items.

Figure 7-3. Business leaders work hand-in-hand with CTSOs. Photo courtesy of National FFA Organization

Besides helping the public identify members of the CTSO, official dress helps members feel more like "part of the group". Dressing neatly often improves conduct. Most CTSOs encourage members to wear official dress whenever they choose, but at minimum it should be worn when members are "on the job": on official business or engaged in CTSO activities, in a large or small group. This is probably the most obvious time to ensure that members present a good image. Members represent the entire CTSO, and should be willing to present themselves in the best manner possible.

The national or state CTSO's code of ethics or rules may list specific official dress, as well as guidelines for conduct and proper etiquette. If the CTSO has not designated an official uniform, the chapter may choose to establish one for local use. Insignia can usually be obtained from a national office and attached to lightweight jackets or blazers, which can then be completed with matching trousers, skirts, shoes, ties, and scarves.

Classroom discussion of group identity can have a positive and immediate impact, but it may be necessary at times for the advisor to discuss this matter individually with a member. Utilizing a checklist listing the criteria for good grooming and uniform wear can be a good place to start. It may be prudent to attend to these topics in a "gender-specific" context (i.e., for a male teacher or resource person to address male students, and a female teacher or resource person to address female students).

Figure 7-4. Well-groomed and appropriately-dressed members project a positive image for the CTSO. Photo courtesy of FCCLA, Inc.

63

Naturally, the advisor should also provide a positive example to members: dressing neatly and practicing good grooming and personal hygiene. The advisor should also conduct him or herself in a professional manner, actively supporting school administration and other activities, and having a good word for others and their efforts.

If a small group of members represents the entire chapter at an event, it would be appropriate for them and the advisor to discuss and present the reasons for the activity and the values behind it. This small group of members should also be called upon to report on their experience to the chapter, including an accounting of relevant finances.

Figure 7-5. Committee work is an important tool for developing a successful public relations program. Photo courtesy of the National FFA Organization.

It is usually best to involve as many chapter members as possible in an activity. Through active involvement, members learn more about the CTSO and its goals. The same can be said about those outside the chapter: greater involvement by parents, teachers, other students, and community members serves to inform the public about the CTSO.

3. CREATING A POSITIVE PUBLIC IMAGE

An effective public relations program will often involve formation of a chapter committee responsible for planning advertising, displays, newsletters, and the like. The chapter reporter may be assigned to this committee as well.

It should be stressed to all members that they are participants in public relations, whether officially part of the committee or not: they present the CTSO and its activities to the public. It is also helpful to utilize the services of communications and journalism students within the school: while assisting the chapter, they learn more about the CTSO. The chapter will want to recognize these efforts at the annual awards banquet.

4. INFORMING OTHER SCHOOL STAFF

Similarly, all teachers and counselors in the school should know about the CTSO, its goals, and the type of students who could most benefit from membership. They can refer appropriate students to the chapter, and provide assistance when needed.

National and state offices may have informative promotional materials that can be distributed to school faculty and staff, or sections of the CTSO manual or handbook may be copied and distributed. Another effective device is to develop a program to inform an audience about the CTSO: this may be presented at a school assembly or for a group of faculty and staff. Goals, purposes, and other talking points about the CTSO can be featured to best advantage. School counselors in particular should be kept apprised, as they can be very helpful with enrolling interested students in CTE classes.

School administrators should be familiar with the CTSO's purposes and goals for the same reasons as other staff, to provide assistance as needed and to make appropriate referrals for membership. A school administrator's job requires that he or she know what is happening in the school. Any assistance the advisor and chapter can provide will be appreciated (e.g., copies of the POA, budgets, and agendas). To this end, the advisor should identify the person or office in the school in charge of all paperwork, scheduling, and clearance of activities. The advisor should be the key person involved with maintaining relations with administrators. His or her behavior and professionalism advertises the CTSO.

A personal word or note of thanks for helpful efforts by administrators, teachers, and other staff is very reinforcing, and makes it more likely that additional help can be relied upon. Public recognition such as an award is another way to show appreciation, particularly if the occasion is photographed and publicized in the local media.

Generally, good advisors are also respected faculty members that interact positively with other teachers, counselors, and school administrators. Good public relations by CTE students and advisors promote a positive image for the entire school and with the public.

5. INFORMING KEY COMMUNITY GROUPS AND INDIVIDUALS

Through community interaction, the advisor learns which individuals and groups are able to assist the chapter and which will benefit from services the chapter provides. He or she should always be on the lookout for community members and organizations that are willing to help but are not yet familiar with the CTSO.

Community groups and organizations usually welcome the opportunity to make presentations at chapter meetings. Not only does this inform chapter members about the group or organization, but it also provides the community group with information about the chapter, its members, and how meetings are conducted.

Chapter members should be encouraged to make presentations at other groups' meetings as well. This allows the chapter to become visible in the community, and demonstrates the ways that it benefits students. It also provides public-speaking experience, builds presentation skills, and helps the member reaffirm his or her commitment to the CTSO by speaking out about its advantages.

It is wise for the advisor to get to know each member's employer, or potential employer. This helps identify what is expected of members in the workplace, and creates a favorable impression of the CTSO. Potential employers in particular can better understand the purposes of the CTSO's work experience and the kinds of students who will be working with them, and be more inclined to cooperate with the CTSO.
Note that most business people may already have an impression of the CTSO and its work experience program before they are contacted. If the impression is a positive one, the jobs of the advisor and members will be much easier.

Being visible in a positive way is very important. The local chapter is the "face" of the CTSO for most people. One never knows who will come into contact with the CTSO by way of a chapter member or activity: who can provide services for the chapter, or benefit from its work.

6. PUBLIC RELATIONS ACTIVITIES

Many public relations efforts are accomplished easily, when a chapter conducts regularly scheduled activities that include the public. Well-advertised activities promote the chapter. In addition, each CTSO's mission includes public outreach: thus many of its activities and projects involve public service and education. Such activities need to be well advertised before they take place and reported afterward. Local news media are often willing to announce service projects and may even produce a story and photographs on worthwhile accomplishments.

Announcements and news stories should clearly explain how these activities relate to CTSO goals. This makes the public aware of the group's activities, and helps the public associate the CTSO with positive goals and endeavors.

At some time, a chapter may ask the public for financial assistance. Well-advertised *fundraising activities* inform the community about the CTSO while generating income. Most people are willing to support worthwhile educational endeavors. Thus it is imperative that members can explain to potential donors how funds will be used and how this relates to organizational goals.

An *open house* activity allows the public to see and understand more about the CTSO. Such an activity requires significant time and effort by the advisor and members, and thus should be made as valuable and rewarding as possible. Time, date, and location should all be well known by members, their families, and the community. If a chapter activity involves students working at an off-site location (e.g., a workplace, student store, farm, greenhouse, or child care center), the advisor may choose to schedule an open house at this location as well. If this is not possible, the open house may include pictures, bulletin boards, or an audiovisual presentation depicting off campus activities.

The open house is an excellent place to display group projects, with participants' names prominently listed. Awards won by the group should be on display, as well as maps of member job sites and graphics showing job placements. Members should greet visitors at the door, introduce themselves, and offer to answer any questions. The advisor should also be on hand to meet and greet visitors.

Chapter *banquets and award programs* are excellent public relations opportunities. Members' families and other interested people can observe the chapter at its best during these functions. Yearly activities as well as individual and group awards can be prominently displayed. Official ceremonies can provide a description of the CTSO and its goals and purposes. They will also give members public speaking and leadership opportunities, as well as a chance to present a positive, professional image of the CTSO.

Banquets and award programs also provide an opportunity for recognition of members, both individually and in groups, and of community members who have supported the chapter with their time, resources, and effort. Plaques, awards, and public acknowledgement show these individuals that the chapter appreciates them. Local newspapers may be willing to cover these events if they are informed ahead of time. If not, the reporter and the advisor should see that local media are provided with press releases and photos. Award and recognition programs are discussed in greater detail in *Chapter 11: Involvement for Special Needs Students.*

Generally, one week each February has been designated as "National Career and Technical Education Week", and is recognized at national, state, and local levels. CTSOs on all levels, including local chapters, can also *designate their own commemorative days and weeks*, and plan special events and activities to increase awareness of CTSOs. Among the methods used to publicize a CTSO's designated day or week, these have proven successful:

▶ Announcements and articles by the media.
▶ An official day or week proclaimed for the CTSO by the city.
▶ An open house.
▶ Exhibits, posters, bulletin boards, and billboards.
▶ "Uniform Day": the official dress of the CTSO worn by all members on the same day.
▶ A community service project.
▶ A parade.
▶ Letters and information about the CTSO sent to community leaders.
▶ School assemblies.
▶ Distribution of promotional items (e.g., pencils, pens, or other office supplies with the CTSO's name and logo).

Figure 7-6. Inviting the public to an open house allows them to observe first-hand the value of CTSO participation. Photo courtesy of FCCLA, Inc.

With any public relations activity, organization by the advisor and members is the key to success. In every case:

▶ Plan carefully. Make detailed plans for each activity well ahead of time.
▶ Assign a committee to take responsibility for each activity.
▶ Involve as many members as possible.

National and state CTSO offices may provide reference materials that instruct local chapters on how to publicize their activities. Often they can be used "as is", but may also be modified to suit individual chapter needs. The chapter can also review copies of past promotional efforts to get ideas.

Members can use "brainstorming" sessions to develop new promotional concepts. Brainstorming is a method for developing ideas about a particular topic. The members are divided into a number of smaller groups, each designating one of their number as the "recorder". Within each group, all members are encouraged to call out ideas without anyone else questioning or critiquing them. The recorder writes down all ideas presented, and when the larger group reconvenes, all ideas are shared with the entire group for evaluation and feedback. As mentioned earlier, committees may be assigned for each major activity. A suggested list of public relations committees is provided below.

▸ **Publicity:** responsible for newspaper, television, radio, and website announcements. Spot announcements and news stories may be available for free as a public service; the committee and chapter may determine whether purchase of additional media coverage is warranted.

▸ **Special events:** responsible for events such as social and informational presentations to civic groups and other school and community organizations.

▸ **Exhibits, posters, and bulletin boards:** responsible for obtaining and producing graphic displays, and planning and setting up exhibits. These can be placed within the school or in the community (e.g., in a library or shopping center).

▸ **Promotional items:** responsible for obtaining "hand-out" items that promote the CTSO (e.g., pens, pencils, stickers, buttons, t-shirts, or mouse pads). The national or state CTSO may provide these items at reasonable cost. This committee may also choose to create their own items (e.g., flyers, cards, and inserts for community publications).

Figure 7-7. An awards program that recognizes members for outstanding accomplishments is an excellent public relations activity. Photo courtesy of FCCLA, Inc.

7. DISPLAYS

As described above, *displays* can vary in scale from bulletin boards and display cases in a school building to exhibition booths at a convention or shopping center. The advisor may choose to assign a committee to prepare each display: planning the theme, colors to be used, and other details. If possible, another committee can be used to produce and assemble the display. If a particular display needs to be attended by a member, this responsibility can be rotated among many to allow several to participate.

Here again, other school departments can be employed to good advantage. The help of art students and teachers should be used whenever possible, and the chapter will want to recognize these efforts at the annual awards banquet. National and state CTSO offices may have materials that can be used in a display as well.

A checklist for planning and evaluating a display is provided in **Figure 7-8**.

CHECKLIST FOR DISPLAYS
(Check the appropriate column)

The Display:

	Good	Excellent	Needs Improvement
1. provides information on the organization...............	☐	☐	☐
2. concentrates on one main point...........................	☐	☐	☐
3. presents one idea clearly and simply....................	☐	☐	☐
4. is neat...	☐	☐	☐
5. is uncluttered...	☐	☐	☐
6. has one focal point....................................	☐	☐	☐
7. attracts attention.....................................	☐	☐	☐
8. uses motion..	☐	☐	☐
9. is appropriate for audience............................	☐	☐	☐
10. has neat lettering....................................	☐	☐	☐
11. uses appropriate colors...............................	☐	☐	☐
12. uses attractive materials.............................	☐	☐	☐

Figure 7-8. Display checklist.

8. MEDIA

The advisor and chapter should learn to use the media: newspapers, magazines, television, radio, local cable access, and the Internet. Since almost everyone obtains information from some type of media, they are public relations tools that cannot be ignored.

Getting to know local editors, broadcast station managers, printers, website developers, and other media professionals is a good start for the advisor. It is important to know the submission guidelines and preferences for each when submitting news and feature stories: exact materials needed should be determined, and deadlines should be met. News organizations are deadline-driven in order to present information to the public in a timely manner.

The advisor should also determine which activities the chapter reporter can cover, and which should be attended by a professional reporter. An important exception is the chapter's banquet or awards program: local media members who work with the chapter throughout the year should be invited and acknowledged.

National and state CTSO offices can provide helpful materials (e.g., press releases and media kits). Some can be used as is, or with only minor insertions; others require significant input of information.

It is essential to learn to prepare articles, press releases, media programs, and photos. Materials that are well done are far more effective than those done haphazardly. As the advisor learns to tell the CTSO's story through the media, he or she can instruct the reporter and other members.

Some basic guidelines for writing a news story are provided below.

- Good grammar, spelling, and sentence structure are absolutely vital. A news article that contains misspellings, grammatical errors, and "typos" looks sloppy and will very likely be "spiked" or tossed.

- All articles – news stories and feature articles – should answer the questions known as the "Five Ws and an H": Who? What? When? Where? Why? and How?

- The first few sentences should summarize the story, and contain the most important facts. This ensures that most readers get the pertinent details, and that important information is not omitted if the story is edited for length. Additional details make up the middle section of the story, and minor details are included in the final sentences. This story structure is referred to as the "inverted pyramid".

- Newspaper articles should be brief and to the point. Remember the acronym "KISS" = Keep It Short and Simple. Feature articles and those for magazines can be lengthier. In either case, it is wise to ask the editor to suggest a word count, and follow it scrupulously.

- Type all news releases and articles, using double spacing throughout. Mastery of a computer's word processing program is essential.

Good photographs improve any news story. Chapter activities provide excellent "photo opportunities". Local newspapers are often eager to receive good quality photos of student activities: in focus and well lit. The advisor should check with local media for their submission requirements. Some guidelines are provided here:

- Show action in photos whenever possible. Pictures of people doing things are more interesting than pictures of people sitting or standing.

- Try to take pictures of no more than three people in a group.

- Get as close to the subject as possible, but make sure the entire scene or group is in the picture.

- Take two or more shots of a set-up, and make sure that one is clear and sharp. Be sure photos are well lit. Color pictures must be exceptionally clear to be reproduced in print.

- Attach a caption to the back of each photo, identifying people, places, the date, and the activity. Do not write on the back of the photo: attach a Post-It note or a piece of paper with tape.

- Mail photos in a heavy cardboard envelope to prevent folds or tearing.

- If submitting digital images, determine the publication's submission requirements. Often a specific format (e.g. TIFF or JPG), resolution (i.e., number of pixels per image), and submission method (e.g., e-mail attachment, diskette, or CD-ROM) will be specified.

- Practice. The more frequently one takes pictures, the better photographer one becomes.

Radio is another popular media available to people at home, at work, in their vehicles, and in public places. People who do not always take time to read an article about a local event will find it easy to listen to the same information on the radio.

The advisor should contact the station manager or program director of local broadcast stations to publicize the chapter. A Public Service Announcement (PSA) should be written and typed like a news story, with double spacing throughout. Again, the national or state CTSO offices may have "copy" available that requires little or no modification, or prerecorded radio "spots" that can be purchased. Chapter members may be asked to come to the studio and record spot announcements to play on the air.

An excellent promotional strategy is to enlist local businesses to develop spots that salute the CTSO. These take the place of regular commercials during special commemorative days or weeks (see above).

Local television can also be an important resource, whether commercial, public broadcast, or public access stations. Most stations have guidelines for accepting programming from service or non-profit organizations. It may be advantageous to contact the national CTSO office to determine if they have video presentations already prepared that can be submitted to local stations. Locally recorded programming can also be submitted, if the school and chapter have the resources available. Here again it may be useful to utilize other school departments. The school media department may be of great help, with appropriate recognition at the annual awards banquet.

Some local stations will be willing to use chapter members as panelists on talk shows. If so, a prepared script should be practiced and submitted to the station for review.

Public access TV, also called cable access, community access, community television, or PEG (Public, Education and Government), provides television production equipment, training, and airtime so the public can produce shows and televise them to a mass audience. Local cable systems are required by Federal law to provide equipment, facilities, and channel space for public, educational, and government programming. Public access is an ideal facility for chapters to keep the community informed about new developments. Chapter members can volunteer to participate in the local public access organization, and learn the basics of video production: story board layout, lighting, camera operation, and studio techniques. Many public access organizations have classes specially designed for young people. In most cases the chapter will receive a copy of all shows produced by members. Here again it may be useful to utilize other school departments: an audio-visual or school media department can be of great help, with appropriate recognition.

All national and some state CTSO offices have developed their own websites to help publicize the organizations. Local chapters may also develop a website that can be linked, with permission, to the state and national sites. Like all public relations activities, a website must be planned and developed carefully; it must also be kept current or it will not be useful to chapter members and other individuals. It is advisable to use a committee to plan and develop a chapter website: one or more members may have the skills needed to develop and post information using the Internet.

Like all media resources a website requires correct grammar and spelling, high-quality photos and graphics, eye-catching colors, and clearly presented messages. Some chapters can utilize the services of a media or information technology department within the school to design and produce a website: the chapter will want to recognize these efforts on the website and at the annual awards banquet.

Reviewing sites that are related to the CTSO's field will provide valuable ideas to help members create the website. It may also be helpful to create a "What's New" page and update it on a weekly or biweekly basis. This page can promote upcoming activities, present recent accomplishments by the chapter or individual members, and provide current information about activities.

Many schools have a website, and student organizations may have the option to place their information on the school's site. In this case, members would work with those responsible for the school's site in creating the chapter's Internet presence.

It is important for the advisor and chapter to keep a file of all public relations activities, noting which are successful and which need improvement. The chapter reporter and historian are usually charged with this responsibility, assisted by the advisor.

CHAPTER 8
Supervising the Financial Operation of the CTSO

All organizations require financial resources in order to operate: a CTSO is no exception. To ensure that a chapter conducts worthwhile activities, providing service and education, it is necessary to acquire funds. And simply having the money may not guarantee that the activities will be conducted. It is necessary to budget to ensure that resources are allocated appropriately and equitably.

Besides keeping the chapter in operation, money management provides a unique educational opportunity for members. Learning where money comes from, how to budget, and keep records are valuable assets for everyone. Finally, a chapter with a well-organized financial plan is much more likely to gain support from school administrators, parents, and community members than one with a more haphazard approach. This section helps the advisor direct members in developing a yearly budget, to distinguish between successful and unsuccessful budgets, and to set a schedule and method for budgeting.

1. DEVELOPING A BUDGET FOR THE YEAR

Developing a yearly budget is not a difficult task, but does require some planning and preparation. The purpose of the budget is to help the advisor and chapter determine how much money is needed to conduct planned activities for the year. A written budget helps determine which activities and operations can be funded by chapter income (e.g., membership dues and fund-raising revenue), and thus ties this income to chapter goals.

The budget should be developed at the beginning of the program year to ensure that funds are available for all planned activities. This approach avoids the awkwardness of developing a budget after funds have already been spent, and having to account for past expenditures. Chapter approval of the budget is best sought prior to the beginning of the fiscal year, when changes and suggestions from members can be easily incorporated. This approach is also helpful for school administrators, and sets a positive tone for the program year. It also provides the advisor with knowledge of the amount of funds needed to run the chapter for the entire year.

The chapter treasurer or another assigned member prepares the budget and keeps financial records, assisted by the advisor. Chapter members, however, develop the actual content of the budget. Many chapters appoint a committee for this purpose, and some appoint a second "auditing" committee to verify income and expenses throughout the year. Input from the membership can be sought at the beginning of the process, or after the budget has been drafted. In either case, the completed budget should be typed, reproduced, and reviewed by the entire chapter for final approval.

A finance committee can review budgets set by the chapter in years past; this helps them establish a framework for the current financial plan. Another good approach is to tie budget line items to their corresponding specific chapter activities. Planning committees can provide a list of expected income and expenses for each activity, and these projections can be submitted to the finance committee for inclusion. A sample budget based upon planned activities is provided in **Figure 8-1**.

The school administration needs to approve the system used by the chapter to account for income and expenses. It is wise to seek instructions from the administration before beginning the budget process; for example, the school may establish guidelines about the location and types of financial accounts the chapter is allowed to maintain.

These suggestions will help maintain an accurate budget:

▸ Membership dues are recorded in the budget as an income source; national, state, and regional dues paid by the chapter on behalf of members are recorded as expenses.

▸ Proceeds from fund-raising activities are recorded as distinct income sources, each as a separate line item. Estimated income should be listed in the budget for each activity based on last year's revenue figures or on the best estimate of the advisor and treasurer.

▸ If the school provides all or part of the chapter's funds, this should be recorded as income in the budget.

▸ All expenses should be recorded in the budget, each as a separate line item. As with fund-raising income, these are estimated in the budget based on the previous year's actual expenditures, the best estimate of the advisor and treasurer, or both.

Note that the projected income and expenses are not likely to balance. While estimates of income and expense need to be as accurate as possible, it is quite difficult to be exact because conditions and circumstances will always vary. A rule of thumb is to be conservative in estimating income, and generous in estimating expenses. "Extra" money at the end of a budget year may be carried over to the next fiscal year (depending upon relevant financial rules), but not having enough money to cover expenses in the current year is unpleasant for all concerned. Therefore the budget should never project a negative balance, and the advisor and members may need to prioritize activities that require funding and eliminate lower priorities if it is not available.

The completed budget should be included in the POA. A copy should also be filed with school administration. This keeps administrators apprised about chapter activities, and enables them to assist when needed.

Accurate financial records must be kept throughout the year. Periodic checks of cash flow help the treasurer and advisor estimate whether expenses match income, and to make necessary adjustments to ensure that priority activities are accomplished. Examples of a proposed budget and one with checkpoints are provided in **Figure 8-2** and **Figure 8-3**.

A successful budget coordinates funds that allow the chapter to accomplish its activities and objectives. The checklist provided in **Figure 8-2** lists some features of a successful budget. A budget that meets all these criteria can be considered beneficial to the chapter; items checked "no" should be amended.

SAMPLE PLANNED ACTIVITIES
Hethwood Health Occupational Student Organization
20XX/20XX

ACTIVITY	Expected Income	Expected Expenses
Booth at fair	$ 15.00	
Toothbrush sale	210.00	100.00
Hospital helpers	320.00	75.00
Banquet	200.00	500.00
Booth at Carnival	300.00	
Operate store	390.00	
Vitamin sale	250.00	100.00
Floral convention	500.00	400.00
Attend state convention		100.00
Attend camp		200.00
Trinity Nursing Home Project		150.00
Collect dues	95.00	
Pay dues to state and national		85.00
Membership pins		100.00

SAMPLE BUDGET
Hethwood Health Occupational Student Organization
20XX/20XX

ESTIMATED INCOME		ESTIMATED EXPENSES	
Dues	$95.00	Local Convention	$400.00
County Fair Booth	15.00	State Convention	100.00
Tooth Sale	210.00	National Convention	75.00
10% of Hospital Helpers	320.00	Camp	200.00
Banquet Tickets	200.00	Trinity Nursing Home	150.00
School Carnival Booth	300.00	Banquet	500.00
Profit of Health Store	390.00	District, State, and National Dues	85.00
Vitamin Sale	250.00	Hospital Workers Uniforms	75.00
Local Convention Registration Fee	500.00	Membership Pins	100.00
		Purchase of Toothbrushes	100.00
		Purchase of Vitamins	100.00
		Miscellaneous	100.00
		Transfer to Savings	295.00
TOTAL **Estimated Income**	**$2,280.00**	**TOTAL** **Estimated Expenses**	**$2,280.00**

Figure 8-1. Sample budget.

CHECKLIST FOR BUDGET

The Budget:

		Y	N
1. is in a written form..		☐	☐
2. excludes departmental operations...................................		☐	☐
3. includes activities related to organizational goals.....................		☐	☐
4. was developed at the beginning of the year................................		☐	☐
5. was developed by students...		☐	☐
6. was developed using member ideas...................................		☐	☐
7. was developed under advisor guidance...........................		☐	☐
8. was approved by the organization..................................		☐	☐
9. was approved by the school administration.............................		☐	☐
10. includes membership dues as income.............................		☐	☐
11. includes all fund-raising activities as expected incomes...............		☐	☐
12. includes each fundraising activity as a separate entry................		☐	☐
13. includes each expense as a separate listing..............................		☐	☐
14. includes each activity planned by the organization................... (and is based on the program of activities)		☐	☐
15. has provisions for periodic checks of income and expenses.....		☐	☐
16. is on file with the administration..		☐	☐

Figure 8-2. Budget checklist.

SAMPLE BUDGET WITH PERIODIC CHECKS
Hethwood Health Occupational Student Organization
20XX/20XX

Activity	Expected Income	Estimated Expense	Actual Income As of Dec. 31	Actual Expense As of Dec. 31	Actual Income As of June 30	Actual Expense As of June 30	Closing Balance (+) (-)
County Fair Booth	15.00		15.00				+$ 15.00
Toothbrush Sale	210.00	100.00		100.00	300.00		+ 200.00
Hospital Helpers	320.00	75.00	100.00	75.00	220.00	15.00	+ 230.00
Banquet	200.00	500.00			220.00	560.00	- 340.00
Booth at Carnival	300.00		250.00	40.00			+ 210.00
Operate Health Store	390.00		200.00		220.00		+ 420.00
Vitamin Sale	250.00	100.00			270.00	100.00	+ 170.00
Local Convention	500.00	400.00	400.00			400.00	.00
Attend State Convention		100.00		150.00			- 150.00
Attend National Convention		75.00				75.00	- 75.00
Attend Camp		200.00		210.00			- 210.00
Trinity Project		150.00				150.00	- 50.00
Dues	95.00	85.00	95.00	85.00			+ 10.00
Member Pins		100.00				100.00	- 100.00
Miscellaneous		100.00		40.00		20.00	- 60.00
Transfer to Savings		295.00				170.00	+ 170.00
	$2,280.00	$2,280.00	$1,060.00	$700.00	$1,230.00	$1,590.00	

Figure 8-3. Sample Budget

Three hypothetical budgeting situations are described below. The reader should review each one, referring to the budget checklist in Figure 8-3 and other information in this chapter, and determine what is right or wrong with the procedure used for each. Model answers for each scenario are found on page 79.

▶ *Hypothetical #1*

Mr. Penny was a new advisor for a CTSO, eager to do everything correctly and particularly mindful of funding issues. He decided early on to set up a committee of five members, including the chapter treasurer, to develop the annual budget. He provided the group with some blank budgeting forms, with spaces to fill in anticipated expenses and income. Satisfied that the members were learning about the budgeting process, Mr. Penny retreated to his desk to complete some paperwork..

When the completed budget was taken to the chapter meeting, the members were very pleased and unanimously approved it. The committee had planned many fund-raising activities because they wanted to take in a lot of money. Mr. Penny was impressed with how well the group had done, and he and the members were eager to begin their fund-raising activities.

Not long after this Ms. Greenback, the parent of a member, approached Mr. Penny at his classroom desk after school. Ms. Greenback told him that she had looked at the CTSO's budget, and was having trouble understanding all the activities the chapter was planning to conduct during the coming year. "You see," she said, "I enrolled my daughter in this program so she could learn technical skills - not to go around selling toothbrushes, working in a carnival booth, or any other such shenanigans." Mr. Penny was a good listener and a good diplomat. He explained the student-run budget and activity process to Ms. Greenback, and eventually she headed home in a better mood.

As Mr. Penny finished up his business for the day, he noticed an e-mail message from the director of the CTE department reminding all advisors that the assistant principal would meet with them the following day after school. During that meeting, he would distribute budget forms to be used by all CTSOs. The e-mail also listed a due date for the return of the budget forms, and an appointment date for administrative approval of each budget.

▸ *Hypothetical #2:*

Mr. Nickel wanted to try a new approach with his CTSO this year. He had read about how developing a budget could help a chapter run smoothly, and here it was three months into the school year before he had a chance to try it. Many of the chapter's recurring annual activities had already been completed when Mr. Nickel finally sat down with the treasurer and finance committee, and try as they might; they had difficulty recalling all the activities that had already occurred!

Eventually the committee remembered all the chapter's activities, but a new problem emerged: recalling the income and expenses associated with each one. "Well, we have to do something," Mr. Nickel told the group. "Let's just lump all the income so far this year into one figure, all the expenses into another, and submit them like that."

The committee finally set up the budget, filed a copy with the school administration, and placed a copy in the POA. Mr. Nickel was pleased with the results, and was convinced that a formal written budget was the way to go for his chapter.

Unfortunately, when they read the budget, a few members began to complain about some of the line items. "Just who set this budget anyway?" one was overheard to ask. "Beats me," replied another. "Probably Mr. Nickel and a few of his teacher's pets. I never saw the thing myself."

▸ *Hypothetical #3:*

Ms. Dollar knew how to handle the finances of any organization. She'd been doing it for years, carrying numbers in her head, and knew that writing down income and expenses was a waste of time. Goodness knows, she had enough to do without any more busywork!

The chapter's treasurer, however, had an idea. He suggested that Ms. Dollar and the chapter president appoint a finance committee to develop the budget. Privately Ms. Dollar knew this idea was for the birds. She had tried that one year, after all, and the students couldn't decide how or when to do anything. Besides, students don't know the goals of the CTSO anyway, she reasoned, so how could they be expected to set a budget? But Ms. Dollar went along with the half-baked idea. "Sure, we can have a finance committee," she cheerfully told the treasurer. "And congratulations! You're the new chairperson!"

The end of the year came and Ms. Dollar made sure the chapter didn't end up in the red. It was a disappointing year for the members, though, as several activities had to be cancelled because there weren't enough funds. "Oh well," Ms. Dollar sighed, "easy come, easy go. We'll do more next year."

Model answers to the three hypotheticals are provided below.

▸ *Model Answer #1:*

Mr. Penny had the right idea when he involved chapter members in preparing the budget. He also remembered to get the budget approved by the membership, and fortunately the students were eager to take part in the activities.

He neglected, however, to provide the guidance that students need. The budget should include funds for activities listed in the POA, which should be developed with the chapter's goals and objectives in mind. As was evident from Ms. Greenback's comments, the students had listed activities with little consideration for the purposes of the chapter.

Mr. Penny also neglected to find out if the school had an established format for budget preparation, and overlooked the need to get administrative approval.

▸ *Model Answer #2:*

Mr. Nickel was on the right track when he decided to develop a written budget, working with the treasurer and a student committee. To be most effective, however, the budget should have been completed at the very beginning of the school year. Grouping all income and all expenses together could lead to trouble if the budget were to be audited. In addition, this approach makes it difficult to evaluate which activities were successful and which were a drain on the budget.

Mr. Nickel was correct to file a copy of the budget with school administration, and place another in the POA. He neglected, however, to seek member approval by reviewing and accepting the budget at a chapter meeting.

▸ *Model Answer #3:*

Ms. Dollar contributed to the problem of leaving out many priority chapter activities by not developing and following a budget. If estimated income and expenses were documented and periodically checked, decisions could have been made to ensure activities took place (for example, additional fund-raising activities could have been initiated). A written budget could also be used in later years for planning which activities to include and which to omit.

Ms. Dollar's attitude about member involvement may have resulted from an experience where members were expected to do all the work themselves, with no guidance. Her members definitely need to know the goals of the CTSO, for then they would be able to set a budget.

She did ensure that the chapter did not overspend. Her system of "carrying numbers in her head", however, could cause difficulty if the chapter was asked budgetary questions by auditors, school administrators, parents, or community members.

2. DUES

Paying dues, or membership fees, is a requirement in most chapters. Being an active member of a chapter requires giving all resources, such as time, energy, and money. It is generally a good practice to expect all members to pay dues in order to participate and be in good standing: in this way, all participants contribute equally. Recognizing that not all members come from equal situations, some chapters develop a method of equivalent work or service whereby members can earn dues payments.

The term "dues" generally encompasses local, state, regional, and national membership fees. In most cases the local chapter determines a "lump sum" figure that encompasses all of these fees, and then all amounts (except local dues) are mailed to the appropriate offices by the advisor, secretary and treasurer.

Active members who have graduated or no longer attend school are required to pay dues as well. Many CTSOs have other levels of membership (e.g., alumni); these members are assessed dues differently from active members, and many chapters require that they pay local dues only.

In many cases, the chapter treasurer needs help collecting dues. One good approach is to assign an individual to collect dues for his or her class, and give these to the treasurer. Another is to offer an incentive for prompt dues payment (e.g., T-shirts, membership pins, or attendance at a chapter party). It is wise for the treasurer and assistants to issue a multiple copy receipt to each dues-paying member.

Members are usually issued a membership card when dues are paid. Many chapters provide discounts at various events when members show their cards.

3. FUND-RAISING ACTIVITIES

Unless a chapter is one of the rare ones that gets all of its financial support from the school, it will undoubtedly be necessary to conduct fund-raising activities. Well-organized and effective fund-raising activities provide not only income but also educational experiences.

Fund-raising ideas can come from many sources. One such source is the official magazine of the national CTSO, such as FFA's *New Horizons*, FBLA-PBL's *Tomorrow's Business Leader*, FCCLA's *Teen Times*, SkillsUSA's *Champions*, and DECA's *Dimensions*. An advantage to using official publications in this way is that the suggested activities are likely to correspond with the goals and objectives of the CTSO.

As described in *Chapter 7: Supervising the Development and Conduct of a Public Relations Program*, "brainstorming" is another effective method for developing fundraising ideas. The members are divided into a number of smaller groups, each designating one of their number as the "recorder". Within each group, all members are encouraged to call out ideas without anyone else questioning or critiquing them. The recorder writes down all ideas presented, and when the larger group reconvenes, all ideas are shared with the entire group for evaluation and feedback.

Note that each school should have a person responsible to oversee fund-raising activities for all organizations. He or she would be a good resource for ideas, and information about activities that have been successful in the past. Also, some schools limit the number of fund-raising activities each club or organization may conduct. The advisor should obtain a copy of the school's fund-raising policies.

Other organizations within the school and community may also provide good fund-raising ideas. It is important, of course, not to duplicate another organization's activity at or near the same time.

Some chapters assign one or more fund-raising committees to select and plan activities, generating ideas from the sources described above. As many members as possible should participate in these committees to generate a large number of ideas. Once generated, the list of ideas should be evaluated according to these criteria:

- Has the activity received official approval from school administration?
- Is the activity worthwhile and educational? Does it provide obvious value, and enhance member knowledge?
- Is the activity consistent with organizational goals and objectives?
- Is the activity consistent with the opinions of the community?
- Does the activity provide a service or value, as well as making money?
- Is the activity "cost-efficient" in terms of time, effort, and money expenditure?
- Does the activity involve every member?

Some suggestions for fund-raising activities include:

- Concession stands at school events.
- Organizing a used book, CD, or software store
- School dances or concerts.
- Building Projects
- Plant and flower sales.
- Wordprocessing Projects
- Gift, card, and stationery sales.
- School farms and greenhouses
- Sales of food items (e.g., cake, candy, or citrus).
- Childcare centers
- First-aid kit, sewing kit, or toothbrush sales.
- Hospital work
- Organizing a school supply store.
- Pledging a percentage of member earnings

After the chapter determines which fund-raising activities to take on, a few more considerations must be made. Some of these are outlined below:

- It is very important to **seek the approval of members**. A fund-raising project's success depends upon the cooperation of all participants. It is wise to bring all ideas for fund-raisers to a vote in a meeting early in the year.

- **Timing is essential**. Even the best-planned activity will fail if conducted at the wrong time.

- As mentioned above, it is important **not to duplicate another organization's activity** at or near the same time. Many schools have a person responsible for overseeing fund-raising activities for all organizations, and posting all activities on a school calendar. He or she can help determine the best time for an activity. Note too that some students may be members of more than one CTSO.

- It is also important **not to "overload" the chapter** with multiple fund-raising activities within a short time period. Members may feel that they have used too much time and energy. Thus, it is important for members to be involved in scheduling fund-raising activities.

- *Develop a specific method for collecting funds*. Each member should know how the method operates, and follow it consistently. It is best to devise a system to collect small amounts of money from students in several collections rather than rely on one or two collections of large amounts during the course of the event.

- *The advisor's work is not done even after the fund-raising activity begins*. He or she must provide reminders and pep talks, help collect money, and monitor cash flow.

4. RECEIVING AND DISPERSING CHAPTER FUNDS

Collecting and spending chapter funds may seem simple, but proper coordination does require effort. Haphazard money handling methods often lead to complications. These guidelines will help the chapter deal successfully with financial issues.

- As is the case with many aspects of organizational activities, the advisor should check with school administration *to determine policies about receiving and disbursing funds*. Some schools leave bookkeeping arrangements to the individual CTSO, while others require all funds to be transferred through a central office.

- In most CTSOs it is the treasurer's job to collect and disburse funds and keep all records. He or she may find it helpful to *assign one or more other members* to collect funds and issue receipts. Note, though, that *the advisor is ultimately responsible for all cash transactions*. Therefore most advisors periodically check the records with the treasurer, particularly during large fund-raising projects. Both the treasurer and advisor should sign all checks or authorizations for checks issued for expenditure of chapter funds.

- *A treasurer's report should be provided at each chapter meeting*. Members should have an opportunity to discuss the report and ask questions regarding the budget.

- In many schools, *an auditor checks the financial records of each organization.* Several steps can be taken to make this task easier for all concerned and simplify the treasurer's reporting responsibilities. These include paying all expenses by check, or by purchase order from the school office; keeping all returned checks or carbon copies of checks; and using receipts with carbon or electronic copies and an official treasurer's book.

- Many schools establish a policy for *ordering supplies* through a central office. Both the advisor and treasurer should be aware of this procedure. If none exists, the chapter may choose to develop their own, and make sure that a minimum number of members are involved in ordering materials. The advisor should approve all requests before orders are placed.

- *Copies of all orders* should be kept in a central file, and can be used to verify accuracy and expedite returns. The advisor and treasurer should be mindful of estimated fulfillment times for orders, especially if supplies are needed by a particular date.

CHAPTER 9
Helping Members Develop and Conduct Award and Recognition Programs

Recognition for a job well done is a powerful motivator. CTSO members who reach individual or group goals deserve recognition for their achievements.

Recognition awards for CTSOs usually focus on instructional program skill areas, leadership activities, outstanding chapter accomplishments, community service, and safety activities. Advisors should promote award programs that stimulate interest in the CTSO's field and its related professions. Note too that award programs can be used to evaluate student progress toward educational goals, much like the degree advancement programs described in **Chapter 6: Helping Members Advance Through the CTSO.**

Figure 9-1. Members and advisors should be recognized for their accomplishments. Photo courtesy of FBLA-PBL, Inc.

1. DESIGNING, USING, AND OBTAINING ACHIEVEMENT AND PROFICIENCY AWARDS

Many award and recognition programs are available on the national and state level. Effective advisors use these programs, adapting them when needed to local needs and situations, and encouraging members to pursue them. Most CTSOs provide literature that describes their award programs; in many cases this literature accompanies the applications for the awards.

Figure 9-2. Achievement awards should be presented when objectives are met. Photo courtesy of SkillsUSA Inc.

Advisors should help individual members set and reach realistic goals in the areas of occupational performance and leadership development. Two means to accomplish this are through establishment and use of achievement awards and proficiency awards

Achievement awards allow the member to compete against an established set of standards. ***These awards are not meant to promote competition between members.*** The member is rewarded when the objectives are met; members "compete against themselves" at their own pace without concern about the performance of others. The advisor's responsibility is to help each members set realistic goals, and to provide the opportunity to meet them.

Achievement awards can be customized to meet the needs of individual CTSOs, chapters, advisors, and members. Even though the award is presented to a member, it can be used to accomplish chapter objectives by building the proficiency of several members in a particular skill set. Likewise, if several chapters show proficiency in a particular skill, the state and national CTSOs benefit.

The creativity and innovation of the advisor and members can be put into play when designing an achievement award program. Note, however, that the award should be based upon the CTSO's corresponding instructional program.

The following are guidelines for developing an achievement award program:

▶ Develop a checklist of ***CTE competencies*** that the advisor expects most members to achieve during the course or school year (e.g., cutting a rafter, preparing a budget, adjusting a carburetor, or running a copy machine).

▶ Develop a checklist of ***competencies needed to develop leadership skills*** (e.g., serving on a standing committee, delivering a two-minute speech, or reciting a part in chapter ceremonies).

▶ Develop a checklist of ***career development activities***, highlighting the opportunities, challenges, and rewards of various careers (e.g., visiting a related business, interviewing two professionals in a related occupation, or reviewing two articles in a trade magazine).

- Develop a safety checklist that lists *criteria for personal and occupational safety* (e.g., handling chemicals safely; passing a safety examination with a score of 95% or higher; operating equipment safely in the school shop or laboratory; or reviewing two articles relating to safety practices).

- *Inform members about the awards program.* The relationship between the awards and the course of study should be clearly explained, as well as any relationship between the awards and the member's class grade. It is also helpful to point out that employers evaluate their workers on criteria similar to those set up for the award, and that the performance criteria requires time to be spent both in the classroom and out.

- *Monitor progress.* Each member should have a checklist of award criteria for the advisor to initial after each is completed. Some advisors post member progress charts on the classroom wall, reasoning that members may want to see their advancement in relation to others, while other advisors believe this may discourage less advanced members. Use the incentive that is best for the entire group.

- *Present the awards.* When a member is acknowledged for meeting the standards established for a particular award, he or she is motivated to progress toward the next award. An end-of-the-year event attended by family members or other students (e.g., a parent-member banquet or school assembly) is a good time to recognize member accomplishments. Awards can take many forms based upon cost and availability. Certificates, plaques, trophies, or medals are all popular, with different levels of proficiency shown by varying sizes, colors, or material.

- *Program evaluation* is essential to all educational endeavors. Checklists should be reevaluated at the end of each school year to ensure that programs stay current and relevant to the profession.

Proficiency awards recognize members for exceptional accomplishments in progressing toward specific career objectives. These awards involve competition among members at national, state, regional, and local levels. Proficiency awards create interest in the CTSO, the CTE program, and related occupations, and provide a process to evaluate member achievements.

To utilize the proficiency awards program effectively, the advisor should:

- *Become familiar with the awards* sponsored by the CTSO by reviewing literature from the national and state offices.

- *Inform members of awards and monitor their progress* in completing applications for their chosen award areas.

- *Spell out the awards criteria.* The criteria for determining award winners should be clearly defined in writing, and carefully followed. Advisors should explain the selection process and ensure that members understand how it works before they apply for the award.

- *Select local award winners.* A points system works well in evaluating applications, with the total points for each category listed on the member's application form. Use of a committee is also an effective means for evaluating applications. The committee may include past award winners, school administrators and faculty, members of the advisory committee, community and civic leaders, and former chapter members.

Figure 9-3. Proficiency awards are based on occupational skills learned through participation in CTE programs. Photo courtesy of SkillsUSA Inc.

While it may appear self-evident, note that awards should be provided only to deserving applicants. Diluting the award standards may cause the awards to lose their prestige, and discourage members from competing. It may also be wise for larger chapters to present awards by class or grade level, and then select an overall champion from among the winners. All overall winners would then be promoted to the district, state, or regional level, or other appropriate next tier of competition.

Financial limitations should be the only constraint on the number of awards a chapter can provide. All awards must be based on chapter goals, however, and evaluated using consistently high standards.

Chapter award programs are used to motivate members to join together and work toward common purposes. Members establish group goals and implement procedures to attain them. Some examples of these are community service programs, outstanding chapter programs, and safety award programs. While many of these originate in the local chapter, some national and state CTSOs sponsor award programs that recognize excellence in these areas. The advisor should check with the appropriate national or state office to determine guidelines and application processes.

Community service programs fulfill several purposes: improving the local community, helping members to build their leadership and citizenship skills, and making the CTSO visible in a positive way. Various types of community projects should be considered, and a selection made based upon member interest and community need. Community leaders and groups should be involved in the planning process, as should the local media. Most importantly, encourage as many members to participate as possible.

Responsibilities should be divided fairly, with a chairperson selected to coordinate the effort. Multiple-year projects should be divided into yearly phases that allow different groups of members to be recognized for their achievements, and that permit periodic evaluation of progress. Members should attend community meetings that relate to the project, and invite community leaders to speak with the chapter.

Outstanding chapter programs recognize efforts that relate to the chapter's POA. This recognition encourages members to set and achieve higher standards. Success in this area depends upon the efforts of the committees responsible for the chapter's activities. The chapter vice-president, who is usually responsible for all committees, should serve as the coordinator and monitor progress in applying for this award.

An outstanding chapter program award is one of the most difficult to win. Competition is usually very high, and the quality of applications is very good. It can be one of the most rewarding achievements for the chapter and advisor, however. It is usually a good practice for every chapter to apply for recognition as an outstanding chapter.

Safety award programs create and maintain awareness about potential hazards. Most career and technical programs require that students work with or around potentially dangerous equipment and materials. Accidents can be reduced and sometimes eliminated by creating an awareness of safety precautions: this should be part of the instruction for every occupation or career. A safety award program promotes early participation in safety training and habits.

Safety programs should emphasize the hazards commonly found in the occupations for which members are being trained. Many general safety activities can be the basis for a chapter's safety program (e.g., posting hazard hints in the laboratory, conducting home safety programs, or teaching the safe handling of chemicals and flammable materials). Some CTSOs provide safety applications and guidelines that can be used by the chapter and advisor.

Figure 9-4. Safety should be emphasized in all aspects of career and technical education. Photo courtesy of SkillsUSA Inc.

2. DEVELOPING AND CONDUCTING BANQUETS AND OTHER RECOGNITION ACTIVITIES

The most visible aspects of an achievement or proficiency award program are the activities wherein members receive recognition, credit, and publicity for their accomplishments. Some recognition activities used regularly by CTSOs include:

▸ Parent-member banquets.
▸ Special chapter meetings.
▸ School assembly programs.
▸ Open house activities.
▸ Picnics, barbeques, or other recreational activities,

A recognition banquet is one of the most popular options as it affords the chapter an opportunity to acknowledge members, recognize other individuals, and promote the CTE program. A well-organized, effectively presented banquet is also an excellent way for chapter members to develop and utilize leadership skills.

Careful planning is essential for a successful banquet: ensuring that "last minute rushes" are avoided, and eliminating mistakes and errors that may reflect poorly on the CTSO. It may be helpful to appoint a committee to plan and organize the banquet. Some chapters may assign a special committee, while others may use one of the standing committees (e.g., a public relations committee). Either way, input from other standing and special committees should be sought and utilized. The executive committee should be kept apprised and involved in all banquet arrangements.

The *banquet date, time, and place* should be determined as soon as possible, no later than the second chapter meeting of the school year, and placed on the chapter calendar. The location should be determined no later than the third meeting. Select a date close to the end of the school year; an hour that coincides with family work schedules and dinner hours; and a location that provides adequate space, offers a decorous presentation, and meets with school administration approval. Note that a banquet held in a hotel or restaurant is often costly, and beyond the budget of many chapters.

Checklists should be developed for all groups with banquet activities. Sample checklists are provided in Figure 9-5a and 9-5b: these include all major items that should lead to a successful banquet. Each advisor should maintain a banquet checklist as well, and take steps to ensure that all items are completed. Some suggestions for *preparing the program* include:

▸ *Involve as many members as possible* to serve as speakers, greeters, narrators, masters of ceremony, entertainers, and so forth. The advisor's role in the actual program should be minimal. As with all CTSO activities, the members should run the program with the advisor providing sound advice and counsel.

▸ *Develop and review a script,* including everything to be said in the program. The advisor and executive committee should develop the script together, and the chapter should rehearse it several times before the banquet.

▸ Chapter officers should *memorize all official recitation parts* in ceremonies included in the banquet program. Practice is essential in conducting effective opening, closing, and officer installation ceremonies.

▸ *Establish a time limit for the featured speaker.* A recommended length is fifteen to twenty minutes. Substituting a presentation that features member accomplishments is a good alternative to enlisting a featured speaker.

▸ *Limit the total time of the banquet* to two hours if possible. Make sure that the banquet starts at the scheduled time, and that all members inform their guests of this. Rehearsal of the program will help set a realistic banquet time. Note, however, that a rushed presentation can be as disastrous as a slow, dragging one.

▸ *Assign seating.* Generally, members sit with their parents; place cards may be set up to ensure that all have a seat. School board members, visiting teachers, and other groups can be seated at their own table.

BANQUET PLANNING CHECKLIST

PLANNING/COORDINATING COMMITTEE:

Chairperson: _____

	Estimated Completion Date	Item Completed	Reviewed By Advisor
Banquet Date Selected	_____	_____	_____
Location Selected...	_____	_____	_____
*Banquet Listed on School Calendar..	_____	_____	_____
All Checklists Reviewed Eight Weeks Prior to Banquet.............................	_____	_____	_____
*All Checklists Reviewed Four Weeks Prior to Banquet.........................	_____	_____	_____
All Checklists Reviewed Two Weeks Prior to Banquet..............................	_____	_____	_____
*Final Arrangements Completed..	_____	_____	_____
Write Final Committee Report..	_____	_____	_____
Report Accepted by Chapter...	_____	_____	_____

EXECUTIVE COMMITTEE

Chapter/Club President: _____

	Estimated Completion Date	Item Completed	Reviewed By Advisor
Planning/Coordinating Committee Appointed..	_____	_____	_____
Planning/Coordinating Chairperson Appointed..	_____	_____	_____
Date and Location Approved by Chapter..	_____	_____	_____
Banquet Program Outlined..	_____	_____	_____
Speaker Selected and Approved by Chapter..	_____	_____	_____
Speaker Confirmed..	_____	_____	_____
Script Prepared for Banquet Program...	_____	_____	_____
Review Planning and Coordinating Committee Reports...............................	_____	_____	_____
Prepare Banquet Programs and Have Printed...	_____	_____	_____
Order Awards, Gifts, Decorations, and Supplies...................................	_____	_____	_____
Secure Entertainment..	_____	_____	_____
Prepare List of Award Recipients...	_____	_____	_____
Prepare List of Award Presenters...	_____	_____	_____
Notify Presenters of Duties and Provide Script.....................................	_____	_____	_____
Public Address System Secured..	_____	_____	_____
Practice Sessions Conducted...	_____	_____	_____
Thank You Notes to Individuals Assisting with Banquet.............................	_____	_____	_____
Write Final Committee Report..	_____	_____	_____
Report Accepted by Chapter/Club..	_____	_____	_____

Figure 9-5a. Banquet Planning Checklists

MEAL FUNCTION COMMITTEE:

Chairperson: _____

	Estimated Completion Date	Item Completed	Reviewed By Advisor
*Select Cooks...	_____	_____	_____
*Select Serving Crew...	_____	_____	_____
Develop Menu...	_____	_____	_____
*Review Menu with Cooks..	_____	_____	_____
Provide Committee with Menu.....................................	_____	_____	_____
*Estimate Number Attending..	_____	_____	_____
*Arrange for Ordering Food..	_____	_____	_____
Arrange for Eating Utensils...	_____	_____	_____
Select Serving Style...	_____	_____	_____
Arrange for Recognition of Cooks and Serving Crew....	_____	_____	_____
*Arrange for Clean-Up Equipment...............................	_____	_____	_____
(brooms mops. trash containers, truck, etc.)			
Assign and Notify All Clean-Up Crew Members of Duties.........	_____	_____	_____
Arrange for Tables and Chairs.....................................	_____	_____	_____
Set Up Tables and Chairs..	_____	_____	_____
Arrange to Take Down Tables and Chairs.....................	_____	_____	_____
*Return Any Borrowed Items.......................................	_____	_____	_____
Write Final Committee Report.....................................	_____	_____	_____
Report Accepted by Chapter/Club...............................	_____	_____	_____

PUBLICITY COMMITTEE:

Chairperson: _____

	Estimated Completion Date	Item Completed	Reviewed By Advisor
*Prepare Guest List...	_____	_____	_____
Prepare and Address Invitations..................................	_____	_____	_____
Mail Invitations..	_____	_____	_____
Develop Guest List (persons accepting invitations)......	_____	_____	_____
*Prepare Final Guest List..	_____	_____	_____
Decorate Banquet Facilities...	_____	_____	_____
*Arrange for Photographer for Banquet........................	_____	_____	_____
*Invitations Mailed to News Media..............................	_____	_____	_____
*List of Award Winners Prepared for News Media........	_____	_____	_____
*Banquet Program Available for News Media................	_____	_____	_____
*Review Guest List for Special Invitations...................	_____	_____	_____
(Honorary members School Board members, Teachers, Administrators, etc.)	_____	_____	_____
Write Final Committee Report.....................................	_____	_____	_____
Report Accepted by Chapter/Club...............................	_____	_____	_____

*Advisor should be especially careful in reviewing these items.

Figure 9-5b. Banquet Planning Checklists

Banquet components and program items are largely a matter of individual preference. The following are suggestions for structuring a banquet and program. Note that all participants should rehearse and deliver their spoken parts from memory, being mindful to pronounce the names and titles of all guests correctly.

▶ *Opening ceremonies*, with official recitation parts by chapter officers, are an impressive start.

▶ The *welcome* is presented by a member, and should acknowledge and thank school administration, parents, and community members for their support. It should be no more than two to three minutes in length.

▶ A parent or other community member presents the *response*. It should be no more than five minutes in length.

▶ *Introduction of parents* allows each member a chance to speak before the group. While a meaningful part of the program, it can have two drawbacks: the time required, and the fact that some members will attend without their parents. The time factor can be mitigated, however, by asking all in attendance to hold their applause until all introductions have been made. Allowing members the option of introducing themselves can alleviate the issue of non-attending parents. Another approach is to ask all parents to stand together and be introduced as a group.

▶ It is wise to assign one member to *introduce all guests* (other than parents), asking all in attendance to hold their applause until the end. If many guests are being recognized, it is also a good idea to group their introductions together (e.g., school administrators, school board members, employers, and business representatives).

▶ A younger member can offer an *invocation*. It is a good idea to check with school administrators to determine any guidelines for an invocation.

▶ The *meal* can be served buffet-style, or by servers to individual tables. Either style is acceptable and can be determined by the chapter's preference. Buffets generally involve higher food costs, while meals served to tables involve greater personnel cost and more time. Some chapters ask members to provide some food items for the buffet (e.g., salads or desserts). Other chapters are able to ask a local restaurant or catering service to provide an entrée. Other sources may include school cafeteria staff, civic or church groups, or another CTSO in an "exchange". Cooks and servers should be recognized and thanked during the banquet program.

▶ *Entertainment* can be provided while the meal is in progress. Music or other light entertainment is most often appropriate. Note that it is a good idea to use member talent, if they can provide a good quality program.

▶ Some CTSOs hold *honorary member ceremonies* to recognize community members who have aided the chapter. Chapter officers or first-year members can conduct these ceremonies.

▶ The chapter president or the master of ceremonies can introduce the *featured speaker*. The introduction should be brief. As noted above, a time limit should be set with the speaker, perhaps fifteen to twenty minutes. A presentation that features member accomplishments is a good alternative.

▶ The chapter president, previous award winners, award sponsors, or other officers can present *achievement awards*. Recipients and presenters should be seated near the front, avoiding long walks from the back of the room. It may be wise to ask all recipients to stand on one side of the head table and all presenters on the other side. With some rehearsal, this presentation can be effective, impressive, and time-efficient.

▸ The same persons listed for achievement awards can also present ***proficiency awards***. Ample time should be provided to recognize each participant, while still in the shortest time period possible.

▸ ***Outstanding member awards*** may be presented to older members, first-year members, or both. The same presenters can be used, or the advisor may choose to present these top member awards.

▸ ***Installation of incoming chapter officers*** is another appropriate part of the program. This provides recognition for a large group of members at one time. Often there are official recitation parts for both outgoing and incoming officers, which of course should be spoken from memory.

▸ ***Closing ceremonies*** end the program. They can be conducted by the newly installed officers, addressing all in attendance at the official beginning of their term.

A very helpful resource for the advisor is a copy of the previous year's banquet program, with notes made at the conclusion of the event for changes to be implemented in the next one. Evaluation and follow-up procedures are an important conclusion to the banquet, and indeed to all CTSO activities.

A well-run banquet and recognition activity is an excellent public relations event. While the guidelines in this section should help the chapter prepare a successful event, members and advisors alike can make mistakes. The effective advisor minimizes errors and helps members address problems when they occur, treating an error as a "teaching opportunity" and a learning experience. Chapters that learn from their errors are more likely to produce impressive banquets and recognition activities.

Figure 9-6. Official ceremonies are an impressive and important part of member training, and contribute to the chapter's public relations efforts. Photo courtesy of Business Professionals of America.

CHAPTER 10
Instructing Students in Leadership and Personal Development

The major purpose of any CTSO is to help members develop leadership and personal skills that will in turn help them become productive members of society. These factors should be a high priority when the advisor plans the curriculum. Though several methods for incorporating these skills into organizational activities have been discussed throughout the *Handbook*, a more in-depth approach is needed to integrate them into an instructional program. This section shows the advisor ways to instruct students in these essential skills.

Figure 10-1. Learning how to give a presentation is an important part of leadership and personal development. Photo courtesy of FCCLA, Inc.

1. TEACHING, LEADERSHIP, AND PERSONAL DEVELOPMENT

Too often the school curriculum is centered on technical knowledge, and little guidance is given to leadership and personal skills. Such an oversight is a hardship to students in a time when personality and leadership activities play an important role in employment and career advancement. This is especially true for CTE students, many of who will go directly from training into the world of work.

Leadership and personal development means different things to different people. In the *Handbook* a broad definition is used, encompassing any aspect of education that improves a student's personal and social proficiency. Two important competencies within leadership and personal development are *parliamentary skills* and *public speaking skills*, both of which are commonly taught by CTSOs. Separate portions of this section are devoted to each skill. Other areas that are often taught by CTE instructors include:

▶ *Social skills*: Common expectations regarding social activities. Specific topics can include conversation skills, handling introductions correctly, dining etiquette, social courtesy to peers and elders, proper behavior as a guest, and how to write effective messages and notes.

► **Good grooming**: Helping members look their best and dress appropriately for various occasions. As mentioned in *Chapter 7: Supervising the Development and Conduct of a Public Relations Program*, it may be prudent to attend to these topics in a "gender-specific" context (i.e., for a male teacher or resource person to address male students and a female teacher or resource person to address female students). Specific topics can include caring for one's hair, body, skin, and teeth, selecting clothing that fits well, matching clothing to a specific occasion, clothing care, and evaluating one's own dress and grooming.

► **Working with others**: Understanding and accepting other people and their behavior. Specific topics can include individual and group behavior, discussions of tolerance, cultural awareness, interpersonal skills, and teambuilding or working as a group.

► **Personality awareness**: Identifying strength and need areas in one's individual personality. Specific topics can include identifying strengths and needs among one's personal characteristics and work habits, identifying personal development goals, acquiring positive attitudes, and developing initiative.

► **Citizenship**: Determining the rights and responsibilities related to being a member of society. Specific topics can include identifying and assuming the responsibilities of citizenship, respecting and protecting the environment, becoming informed about social and political issues, and expressing one's views constructively.

► **Communications**: Helping members improve their skills and better exchange ideas. Specific topics can include developing interview skills, participating in conversations and discussions, writing letters, telephone etiquette, using computers, e-mail, and the Internet, and writing a résumé.

► **Time management**: Providing members with strategies to help them improve their use of time. Specific topics can include setting goals, establishing priorities, developing "to do" or "daily task" lists, and keeping a personal calendar of events and activities.

► **Money management**: Helping members manage individual finances. Specific topics can include completing and following a personal budget, maintaining a checking account, setting financial goals, and establishing and maintaining good credit.

► **Committee membership**: Becoming an effective committee member or chairperson. Specific topics can include organizing and conducting a committee meeting, evaluating the accomplishments of a committee, recording minutes, and giving a complete committee report.

Figure 10-2. Social activities are a part of everyday life. Members benefit from instruction on how to interact with others. Photo courtesy of DECA Inc.

These are suggestions only. An advisor will need to determine which of these areas of instruction are appropriate for his or her chapter, and may identify additional need areas. The areas that are selected will depend upon what the members have been taught previously and what is being taught concurrently. It is important to determine the skills members need in order to find and keep employment.

The advisor will need resources to use when developing lesson plans. Thousands of books have been written about leadership and personal development, and new ones appear in the market each day. A core list of suggested publications, the "Top Fifty", can be found in **Appendix IV**, p. 129; additional resources can be located by searching the Internet.

Printed materials need not be the only source of information. Every community has a wealth of resource people who can help teach these skills and emphasize their importance (e.g., school board members, municipal leaders, legislative representatives, employers, public relations professionals, and human resources staff). The chapter's school, and other schools nearby, will often feature people who can help teach these topics. The advisor can check with these other instructors to determine who else is teaching specific skill areas, and gain assistance in developing successful lesson plans.

Figure 10-3. Learning how to get along with others on an individual basis is an important social skill. Photo courtesy of the National FFA Organization.

The local school's curriculum guidelines must be consulted when developing a unit that integrates leadership and personal development instruction. Other factors are related to the timeliness of the instruction: a unit on membership skills should be taught early on, while one on job seeking and interview skills can be taught in more advanced classes. CTSO activities can also impact the curriculum. For example, a unit on social skills may be taught before a major banquet, one on parliamentary procedure before a conduct of meetings contest, and one on committee membership before the chapter begins developing the POA.

All instructional areas need to be included in both the short- and long-range curriculum plans for the program. In this way, the advisor can be confident that members are being taught skills that will help them in their careers.

2. TEACHING PARLIAMENTARY PROCEDURE

Parliamentary procedure is a set of rules governing the conduct of meetings. Parliamentary procedure lets everyone be heard, and allows decisions to be made without confusion. It ensures democratic rule, flexibility, protection of rights, a fair hearing for all, and can be adapted to fit the needs of the CTSO. An important skill for those participating in chapter meetings, parliamentary procedure instruction also prepares members for responsibilities later in life. It is essential that they receive instruction in these skills as early as possible. Beginning advisors often try to teach members too much about parliamentary procedure. Note the similarity,

however, between learning parliamentary skills and a new language: neither should be taught all at once. The basic goal in teaching parliamentary skills to members is to ensure that during meetings:

▸   Agenda items will be addressed one at a time.
▸   Each member will receive courteous treatment.
▸   The rights of the minority will be protected.
▸   The rule of the majority will be followed.

Members will not need to know every part of ***Robert's Rules of Order*** to accomplish these things. Instead, the advisor will need to identify and teach the basic information necessary to accomplish chapter business as efficiently as possible. ***Robert's Rules*** is best used as a dictionary would be: referred to for occasional support after a basic "vocabulary" of procedure has been developed and utilized.

A good resource is the national CTSO's national parliamentary procedure competition. Rules and regulations are reviewed by experts in the field, and should give the advisor an idea about what basic information should be taught. Other texts are available that summarize parliamentary rules. Community leaders can also be helpful in pinpointing and focusing on necessary rules.

Like other skills, parliamentary skills become rusty if not practiced. For that reason, a short review should be provided to the chapter each year. Officers and other students in advanced classes may choose to study parliamentary procedure in greater depth (e.g., rules for national and state meetings).

Note that ***Robert's Rules*** and other parliamentary guides are only that...guides. Members should understand that no parliamentary rule takes precedence over one established by the local chapter.

As mentioned above, one purpose of parliamentary procedure is to ensure that members handle only one item of business at a time. The same principle applies when teaching parliamentary procedure: skills should be taught one at a time to minimize confusion and to allow students to practice a skill until it is mastered. The advisor must present the information needed to develop a particular parliamentary skill. With a main motion, for example, members need to understand the purpose of the motion, its order of precedence, the type of vote required, whether it is amendable or debatable, and if it can be reconsidered. They will also need practice in presenting and handling main motions.

Each member needs to be included in practice sessions. Some classroom teachers assign students as the chairperson or president of the classroom on a rotating basis (e.g., random selection). This gives students experience both in presenting motions and disposing of them as a presiding officer.

Practicing parliamentary procedure can be effective and enjoyable when structured as a competition. A class can be divided into teams, with each team carrying out a parliamentary process. The advisor and other students can serve as judges. Regional, state, and national CTSO parliamentary procedure contests provide further opportunity to develop these skills.

Contests allow members to practice and refine their skill in conducting meetings by presenting, discussing, and disposing of motions properly. Members are required to prepare and approve minutes, present and accept committee reports, and correctly handle a meeting agenda. These competitions also provide valuable experience in public speaking. Contests can include either written or oral questions, or both, about parliamentary procedure; these can motivate more diligent study of the rules of parliamentary law.

In preparing members for competition, consider these guidelines:

▸ All eligible members should have the opportunity to participate. Thus practice sessions should take place during class time, with final preparations made during an evening session.

▸ The advisor should pause the practice sessions at appropriate points to identify mistakes and reinforce correct procedures. An agenda, or order of business, should be set for members to follow. Topics chosen should be those of interest to members, including current and somewhat controversial issues, to enhance discussion and promote realistic and meaningful learning.

▸ It may be helpful for the competition team to rehearse and perform in front of a school or community group. Many chapters present parliamentary procedure demonstrations at school assemblies, civic club programs, and meetings of other organizations.

▸ Clearly defined criteria should be established for selecting members to the competition team. It may be helpful to post a chart with the "running" scores from each practice session, showing who is chosen and why.

3. TEACHING, SPEECH-WRITING, AND PUBLIC-SPEAKING SKILLS

An important part of the CTE student's education is learning to speak in public. The advisor therefore must incorporate public speaking into the instructional program, most likely into every course taught. Some classes may require very involved instruction, and others the requirement of giving an oral report.

Speakers of all ages need practice. An effective starting exercise is to ask all beginning speakers to stand before the group and recite a statement in unison, such as the CTSO's creed. This can be followed by a short oral report on a topic of interest in the field of CTE. The next step is to prepare a short formal speech with instruction on how to identify a topic, research and gather information, and organize and present the text.

New advisors often make the same mistake with public speaking as they do with parliamentary procedure by trying to teach too much of it. While important, such considerations as breathing techniques, diction, and inflection can best be saved for a time when members have advanced and gained more confidence. Several excellent reference books exist, including many listed among the "Top Fifty" in the Appendix.

Each member should be required to complete the speaking assignments. Many will need special help and encouragement including, but not limited to, students with special needs (see *Section 11: CTSO Involvement for Special Needs Members*). The wise advisor will assign grades based not only upon the finished product but also upon improvement over time.

CTSO contests and activities provide excellent opportunities to develop speaking skills, and should be incorporated into the instructional plan. Many CTSOs have both "prepared" and "extemporaneous" speaking competitions. Also, "creed speaking" is a competitive event wherein members recite the CTSO's creed before a panel of judges and answer questions about its meaning. Job interview contests, sales presentation demonstrations, forums, and debates are other activities in which members can gain speaking experience. For all speech competitions, the advisor should:

- Help members identify topics, and suggest relevant reference materials.
- Review and critique the written texts, and evaluate members' delivery.
- Include instruction in motivational speaking and summarization skills.
- Review the rules and regulations of all speech events with the members.
- Provide recognition for outstanding performance.

Scorecards from competitions can be used to evaluate members as they deliver speeches in a class or meeting.

Local contests can be established to select chapter participants for advanced competition. Special awards can be provided as well (e.g., plaques, trophies, certificates, or official apparel). Consider offering awards for the most improved speaker, the most informational speech, and the most inspirational speech.

Members should be encouraged and assisted in making presentations at civic meetings, school assemblies, and other activities. This not only develops members' speaking ability, but also serves as an excellent public relations tool for the chapter.

CHAPTER 11
CTSO Involvement for Special Needs Members

Students with special needs are entitled to education in a setting that is suited to their learning requirements. CTSOs are part of the educational program. Thus, the advisor is responsible for involving students with special needs in the local chapter.

The Vocational Education Amendments of 1968, the Rehabilitation Act of 1973, the Education for All Handicapped Children Act of 1975, and the Educational Amendments of 1976 provide the legal basis to provide CTE programming for all students. Though not directly applicable to education settings, the Americans with Disabilities Act (ADA) of 1990 pertains to this discussion as well, particularly as it applies to the workplace.

Many CTSOs make a concerted effort to include and encourage students with special needs. Wise advisors strive for a membership that represents the entire school population; ideally, this means that the chapter will be made up of students with diverse ability levels. Unfortunately, many other organizations are content to proceed without including under-represented populations. In the middle ground are advisors and chapters that do not actively discourage students with special needs, yet fall short of actually encouraging their participation and modifying programs to meet their needs. Omission of special needs students, however unintentional, may occur for a number of reasons:

▶ Advisors may be reluctant to acknowledge that they hold a social prejudice about a particular group of students. It would of course be ideal to work with a group of students with average or above-average intelligence, values similar to those of the advisor, and no physical or personal problems. Like most ideals, however, this will probably never be achieved; people's circumstances vary widely in any group. The advisor must recognize that fact and look beyond his or her preconceptions to identify positive traits in all potential members.

▶ Students without special needs, particularly in adolescence, may have prejudices about anyone who is "different" from the norm in any way. In fact, some students (and others in society) hold unfair stereotypes of CTE students as a group. The advisor is responsible to help members accept students with special needs. It may in fact be a "teaching opportunity" to discuss unfair stereotypes, and how it may feel for CTE students themselves to be the subject of an undeserved bias. Some members, on the other hand, may have especially positive attitudes toward students with disabilities; the wise advisor will work with these members to welcome and encourage those with special needs. As these students join the ranks, participate, and excel, the full membership will see the value of more open participation.

▶ Communities also carry some prejudice. The CTSO is an excellent place to begin overcoming these biases. As community members see how well students with special needs fit into the chapter, they will find it easier to recognize positive qualities.

Prejudice stems from a lack of understanding and a lack of knowledge. Advisors, members, and citizens alike need to know and understand that students with special needs can be valuable chapter members. Every member contributes to the group; students with special needs share the same capability to contribute as traditional or able-bodied members.

Just as advisors and CTSOs may not know how to involve students with special needs, so too the students themselves may not know that they are welcome and will be accommodated. Advisors and other school personnel are often busy, and unfortunately may not have the time available to promote the CTSO to students with special needs.

Suggestions in this section are not meant to be the final authority. The advisor and chapter members will undoubtedly come up with their own ideas about how to involve under-represented student populations. This chapter provides information about students with special needs, and how to encourage their participation in each activity. It also describes activities a chapter may provide, and modifications that can be made to accommodate students with special needs.

1. WHO ARE STUDENTS WITH SPECIAL NEEDS?

For years, educators have used the words "deprived", "disadvantaged", "physically challenged", "differently-abled" or "handicapped" to describe students who require accommodations not shared by the majority. The US Congress' 1968 amendments to the Vocational Education Act of 1963 (described in *Chapter 1: Relationship of CTSOs to the Total CTE Program*) define a "disadvantaged" person as one with academic, socioeconomic, cultural, or other limitations that prevent him or her from succeeding in a regular occupational program. To reflect both of these definitions, the *Handbook* uses the term "student with special needs". These students are those that have special requirements because of a social, physical, mental, or psychological difficulty.

The characteristics listed for students with special needs may range from minor adjustment difficulties to major impediments. Note that not everyone who fits into one of these categories will require additional modifications or extra encouragement in order to participate. Listed below are groupings of students whose conditions have been characterized as "special needs".

▸   Those with physical, psychological, developmental, or learning disabilities.
▸   Those with social, cultural, or language differences from those of the dominant culture; these students may be referred to as "English Language Learners".
▸   Those with mental or psychological difficulty, including those in active, ongoing recovery from chemical dependency.
▸   Those with personal, home, or emotional problems.
▸   Both underachievers and gifted students may have special needs. Programs meant for large groups of students may fail to address those well above or below a median point.
▸   Others whom the advisor can identify and verify by working with special education teachers at the school.

Before continuing through this chapter, the advisor may want to make a list of students who could be considered to possess special needs, particularly those who are not in a CTE program. Consulting a school guidance counselor or special education teacher can provide names of students with special needs who could possibly benefit from membership in the CTSO.

2. WHAT DOES THE CTSO OFFER STUDENTS WITH SPECIAL NEEDS?

Note that the benefits that a CTSO offers to students with special needs are in most cases the same as those offered to all students.

The CTSO serves as a tool to involve students in a CTE program. Members may join to learn about a particular profession, to socialize with peers, or to have fun. Later they begin to understand how the total education program can be of benefit. In addition, CTSO membership leads to participation in other school activities; and in turn grades, attendance, and attitudes generally show improvement.

Many students learn better in a structured atmosphere; those with special needs are no exception. An effective CTSO has a structured way of conducting its business, operations, and activities.

Participation in the CTSO, with its emphasis on "doing", can allow students with special needs an opportunity to learn their capabilities. Setting personal goals, reaching them, and setting more advanced goals provides quantifiable evidence of a student's accomplishments.

Figure 11-1. Hands-on experience allows members to see that they can succeed. Photo courtesy of SkillsUSA Inc.

The opportunity to try and succeed at a new behavior, "the dignity of risk", is important to everyone. Students with special needs may not have had many such opportunities. In a CTSO, each member is given some responsibility, often starting small and progressively increasing.

Socialization is important to most individuals. A CTSO provides social opportunities and informal contacts in an environment more relaxed than that of a classroom. Activities are usually casual and enjoyable, providing a break from stress.

Unlike other school endeavors, CTSO activities can be molded to fit the member's capabilities, engage other skills besides reading and writing, and often permit the member to compete only against him or herself.

Development of leadership skills is a major function of the CTSO through planning, organizing, and speaking opportunities. These opportunities may be denied to students in many other settings.

As in every aspect of life, cooperation is essential if a CTSO is to succeed. The CTSO teaches cooperation to its members in big and small ways through all aspects of its operation.

3. ENCOURAGING STUDENTS WITH SPECIAL NEEDS TO JOIN

Often it is not an easy task to promote the CTSO among students with special needs. Some such students have had negative experiences with other ventures, others do not feel welcomed by or on an equal footing with current members, and still others simply do not know about the CTSO.

A good public relations program (as described in *Chapter 7*: *Supervising the Development and Conduct of a Public Relations Program*) can help address these issues. Presentations and other promotions reach students with special needs in the same way they reach other students. If the chapter currently has members with special needs, they can serve as role models to others. These members should be encouraged to take a significant role in presentations, and awards they earn should be publicized to the entire school.

Obstacles that may hinder students with special needs from joining can be uncovered by interviewing current and potential members.

As mentioned above, counselors, teachers, and school administrators may be able to recommend students with special needs for membership.

The advisor may want to keep track of how successful recruitment efforts are among students with special needs. Such record keeping may be required to qualify for various programs or funds, and the advisor may also want to keep school administrators, teachers, and counselors apprised of these students' progress in the CTSO.

The POA is an excellent opportunity to track member participation, since each member will usually be required to participate in at least one chapter committee. As students with special needs get more involved and become chairpersons, their names and accomplishments will become more and more prominent. Photos and reports of such students serve many functions: they reinforce the students, inform the community about these students' involvement, and provide positive recruitment opportunities.

4. ACCOMMODATIONS THAT PERMIT PARTICIPATION BY STUDENTS WITH SPECIAL NEEDS

For the safety of all participants, *it is critical that all school regulations prohibiting drug and alcohol use and violent, threatening behavior are clearly posted and rigorously enforced without exception.* All members, especially those with special needs, must be able to rely upon a safe and chemical-free learning environment.

In addition, these modifications have been used successfully by CTSOs to accommodate the participation of members with special needs.

▸ Use smaller groups, rather than larger ones, for work tasks.

▸ Individual work, when practical, allows members to work at an individual pace. This is a key to success for many with special needs.

▸ Safety modifications may be needed for a member with a physical, psychological, or developmental disability. Check with school administrators or state directors of CTE to determine needed safety precautions. Therapists, counselors, and psychiatrists can also help modify activities to meet member needs.

▸ Peer assistance is meaningful to many members with special needs. Members who have overcome hardships or disabilities can mentor others in similar situations. Similarly, other members can also excel at mentoring those with special needs. Helping skills, like other work and life skills, can be learned.

▸ Structure activities by breaking them down into tasks with small successes. Many students who have failed often will be encouraged by early success.

▸ Reduce financial pressure on members. Those with limited resources deserve to participate in activities like all others. As mentioned in *Chapter 8: Supervising the Financial Operations of the Chapter*, some chapters provide a type of work or service whereby members who cannot afford to pay dues can earn them. Members can also be allowed to earn points toward trophies or awards by providing services that require no money.

▸ Involve parents and community groups (e.g., civic and benevolent organizations, church outreach groups) in CTSO activities.

▸ Help members evaluate their own progress at each level. Make changes and corrections early, and reward progress.

▸ Rewards are extremely valuable. Note that what rewards one member may not do so for another. It is important to provide appropriate recognition for the achievements of all members as often as possible.

▸ Vary meeting times as able to accommodate more members. Schedule make-up sessions for instruction. Make audio or video recordings of meetings for member review.

▸ Provide transportation options. In some cases, funds may be available for this purpose. It may also be possible for members to car-pool to and from meetings and activities: not only meeting transportation needs, but also social ones.

Participation by students with special needs may not increase all at once; membership may increase by a few at a time. It may be wise for the advisor and chapter to set a yearly goal for increased participation by these under-represented students, evaluating and changing outreach strategies as needed. An evaluation checklist is provided at the end of the text to determine the effectiveness of a chapter's recruitment efforts.

NOTES

CHAPTER 12
Supervising a Yearly Evaluation of the CTSO

An evaluation is a determination of something's value and efficacy. Evaluation of a chapter provides a means to measure its effectiveness. All positive and negative comments from members, advisors, parents, teachers, school administrators, and community members make an evaluation of the chapter. So do observations about particular activities and events, specific members, and the chapter's overall effectiveness.

It is often difficult, however, to translate these candid observations into a cogent, objective format that can help the chapter make decisions. A written evaluation, systematically conducted, provides a clearer picture.

Figure 12-1. Evaluation is important to maintain program support and make informed decisions. Photo courtesy of FCCLA, Inc.

1. THE PURPOSE OF EVALUATION

Perhaps the best reason to determine the value and effectiveness of a chapter is to provide objective feedback to the advisor, school administrators, and community members. Students need to know the chapter's successes, and local business people prefer to offer occupational experiences to members of a valuable chapter. Funding sources, also, look to annual reports to make decisions about whom to support. This feedback informs all concerned parties about the chapter's successes, and helps determine continued levels of support.

Another reason is to identify need areas and take steps to correct them. Continual progress toward long-term goals keeps chapters vital and relevant.

Evaluation can lead to objective decision-making. If an activity is found to no longer meet the needs of the chapter, it can be omitted and replaced by another. A systematic evaluation of two or more alternatives can determine which is better suited to member needs. Similarly, an evaluation may show that an activity is too costly in terms of money, time, or effort in relation to the benefit provided. This may lead to the activity being replaced by one that is more cost-effective. Adopting new and innovative ideas is easier with an objective evaluation in place.

2. ESTABLISHING EVALUATION GUIDELINES

An evaluation project with no established guidelines is like a baseball game with no home plate or base paths: lacking a clear start, finish, and direction. As the saying goes: "If you don't know where you're going, any path will get you there."

Goals and objectives must be set before the advisor and members begin the evaluation. Here it may be useful to distinguish between the two, as the terms are often interchanged. A *goal* is a general statement about what members will gain from chapter participation, not expressed in measurable terms. An *objective* is a more specific, measurable statement that specifies both action and a standard of performance. Continuing the baseball game analogy: the goal is home plate and the objectives are to touch each base on the way there.

Chapter goals and objectives, of course, should be consistent with those of the national and state CTSOs.

Chapter objectives should be specific, measurable, and observable. An objective should clearly state the desired outcome (what is sought), the behavior that will meet the outcome (what is being done), and the threshold of success (how an observer will know when it is completed). In short, ask these questions: where are we going, what are we doing, and how will we know when we're there?

Consider these two objectives:

▸ The chapter will encourage member participation in contests.

▸ At least 90% of chapter members will participate in a local, state, regional, or national contest by the end of the school year.

It is easier to determine whether the second objective was met. It lists the desired outcome (member participation), the behavior (participation in contests), and the threshold of success (at least 90% by the end of the school year). The first objective lacks all these elements: encouraging member participation is nearly impossible to quantify.

Note that objectives should be written in active rather than passive terms. Avoid what are commonly (and humorously) referred to as "dead person's objectives": in other words, objectives that can be achieved by inactivity, without purposeful action. Consider these two objectives:

▸ Chapter members will not spend all chapter funds.

▸ The chapter will disperse its funds to meet all chapter needs, and decrease spending by at least 10% compared to last year.

Apply this test to these objectives: could a dead person achieve it? In other words, could it be met through inactivity? If the answer is yes, it does not pass the test. The first objective can be met through inactivity: a dead person will not spend *any* of a chapter's money, and certainly not all of it. The second passes the test: a decrease in spending while meeting all chapter needs is an observable, measurable action.

3. HOW TO CONDUCT AN EVALUATION

Once goals and objectives are established, the evaluation can begin. Chapter members, school administrators, and the local program advisory committee should be consulted.

Members are in an excellent position to review and evaluate the chapter's accomplishments, examining each activity and its related goals and objectives. A good way to accomplish this is to schedule an end-of-year evaluation meeting with the chapter's executive committee, perhaps combined with a recreational activity.

Member input can be garnered by requiring each POA committee to evaluate specific activities as they occur. The executive committee can then summarize these evaluations and provide a comprehensive report of the year's work.

Some chapters evaluate their activities and accomplishments by comparing them to those of other chapters, usually coordinated by a regional, state, or national office. This evaluation creates a ranking of chapters within the survey area (e.g., excellent, superior, very good, and so on); designations will vary. A committee evaluates the chapters after receiving a standardized application form from each. The advisor is responsible for obtaining the application form and determining the deadline and submission address. Members can complete the form on an ongoing basis, referencing specific activities as they occur through the year. It may be wise to assign one member of each committee to work together on the evaluation form.

School administrators are responsible for monitoring the chapter and its activities, so should be included in the evaluation process. Administrators should meet with the advisor and the executive committee near the end of the school year. Points for the administrators to address should include:

▸ How well did the chapter aid members' educational development?

▸ Did the chapter help the school meet its objectives?

▸ Which chapter activities seemed most important? Which, if any, seemed inappropriate?

▸ What was the chapter's major benefit or contribution to the school this year?

▸ What should the chapter do differently next year?

▸ Was the administration kept apprised about major chapter issues and activities?

In addition, a general discussion concerning the overall program is extremely valuable. Administrators are in an ideal situation to note needed improvements, are inclined to help implement their suggestions, and feel more connected to the chapter when their input is noted.

A *community advisory board* provides feedback concerning the total CTE program, of which the chapter is a part. The advisory board can address the same questions as the administrators, as well as discussing member placement rates and activities related to community employment. While it is likely that the board has been kept apprised of the chapter's activities, it is wise to include a summary of the year's events to ensure that all major issues are covered.

Two methods should be used to conduct the evaluation. One is a continuous, ongoing written evaluation as the year proceeds; the other is an end-of-year summary. The *Handbook* recommends that the advisor utilize both, using the ongoing evaluation to provide information for the summary. Continuous evaluation allows for improvement and course correction before the end of the year (e.g., reducing a shortfall from one fund-raiser by making adjustments during the next).

Evaluation methods can vary according to chapter needs and preferences. *Checklists* often prove the most helpful and easiest to use. Samples that cover most of the operational aspects of a chapter are provided at the end of the *Handbook*. They provide an easy way to evaluate the chapter's activities, and can be modified as necessary.

Follow-up evaluations determine how well the chapter has done over time. It determines what former members are doing, and how well the chapter met their needs. Such evaluations can be completed annually, or every three to five years. Follow-up evaluations allow the chapter to address improvements they may not have learned about if only current members participated.

Figure 12-3. Current and former members should be surveyed as part of the evaluation. Photo courtesy of DECA Inc.

Questionnaires completed by former members often are revealing, Respondents rate the chapter in terms of leadership skills provided, assess attitudes and values emphasized by the CTSO, and rank the chapter activities that made positive contributions to their careers and lives.

Group evaluations are often helpful: whether attendance has increased or decreased, which activities were attended by what members, and what awards were received by the chapter. Sample checklists that tally this data are provided at the end of the *Handbook*. These data, however, do not tell the whole story. Group evaluations do not account for the efforts of all members; many chapter goals and objectives require *individual evaluation* of each member's accomplishments as well as those of the entire group. Individual accomplishment can be evaluated in terms of the number of committees served on, offices held, community service work, and awards won. This can be tracked by each member on individual progress charts, and reviewed by the advisor.

A similar tool is the point system, wherein each activity and accomplishment is assigned a number of points based on time and effort required. Members earn these points by active participation. Extra points can be offered for serving as chair of a committee. The point system has several advantages:

▶ It is objective. Individual evaluation is not subject to a chapter vote or the advisor's subjective opinion.

▶ Points are gained by greater participation throughout the year, rather than involvement in a few activities.

- Members who work better "behind the scenes" on numerous activities are on an even playing field with those who enjoy greater recognition and "limelight".

- It becomes an excellent motivational tool when rewarded by a trophy or prize.

Individual records can serve as individual evaluation. Members who may lack personal and scholastic characteristics benefit from this system: as their participation increases, their records show their progress and allow verification of their accomplishments by themselves, the advisor, and the school administration.

4. WHAT SHOULD BE EVALUATED?

Everything the chapter does should be evaluated for its own sake. It has been said that anything worth doing is worth examining. In addition, state and national CTSO offices may require demographic data regarding chapter activity. The advisor may want to evaluate member knowledge about the principles and purposes of the CTSO, using a written or oral test. This may indicate where additional instruction is needed.

Checklists provided at the end of the *Handbook* help conducting an annual evaluation. These can be tailored to meet chapter needs, and are best used throughout the year on an ongoing basis. Each checklist should address chapter strengths and needs, and help determine which activities to keep, eliminate, and modify.

NOTES

APPENDIX 1
Policy of the US Department of Education (USDOE) for Vocational Student Organizations

The United States Department of Education maintains a close relationship with ten vocational student organizations and welcomes their cooperation and support in strengthening programs of vocational-technical education. Recognizing that the past performance and future potential of these ten organizations are compatible with the overall purposes and objectives of education today, the United States Department of Education strongly endorses their objectives and seeks to involve their thinking in the improvement of vocational-technical education.

In view of this, these policies represent the position of the United States Department of Education:

1.   The United States Department of Education recognizes the educational programs and philosophies embraced by the following vocational student organizations as being an integral part of vocational education instructional programs:

   ▶ Business Professionals of America
   ▶ Distributive Education Clubs of America
   ▶ Future Business Leaders of America – Phi Beta Lambda
   ▶ National FFA Organization
   ▶ Future Homemakers of America
   ▶ Health Occupations Students of America
   ▶ National Postsecondary Agricultural Student Organization
   ▶ National Young Farmer Educational Association
   ▶ Technology Student Association
   ▶ Vocational Industrial Clubs of America

2..   The United States Department of Education recognizes the concept of total student development as being necessary for all vocational-technical education students to assume successful roles in society and to enter the labor market.

3.   The United States Department of Education will facilitate technical and supportive services to assist vocational student organizations through State agencies in their efforts to improve the quality and relevance of instruction, develop student leadership, enhance citizenship responsibilities, overcome sex and race discrimination and stereotyping, and serve students of special populations.

4.   The United States Department of Education recognizes the responsibility for vocational-technical instructional programs and related activities, including vocational student organizations, rests with the State and local education agencies.

5.   The United States Department of Education approves of Federal and State grant funds for vocational-technical education to be used by the States to give leadership and support to these vocational student organizations and activities directly related to established vocational-technical education instructional programs at all levels under provisions of approved State plans for vocational-technical education.

Efforts on the part of State and local education agencies to recognize and encourage the growth and development of these vocational student organizations are highly important and deserve the support of all leaders in American Education.

Signed by Lauro F. Cavazos, Secretary of Education, and Betsy Brand, Assistant Secretary for Vocational and Adult Education, February 12, 1990.

- - -

1.   Now known as DECA.
2.   Now known as Family Career and Community Leaders of America (FCCLA).
3.   Now known as SkillsUSA.

APPENDIX II
Information About the Ten Major CTSOs

The advisor will need to learn background information about relevant organizations. Official manuals, handbooks, and websites are good sources of information. Pertinent information about the ten major CTOs is listed below, complementing the summaries in Section II. Listed in order of their establishment, the organizations are:

▸ FFA
▸ Future Business Leaders of America – Phi Beta Lambda (FBLA – PBL)
▸ Family, Career and Community Leaders of America (FCCLA)
▸ DECA
▸ SkillsUSA
▸ Technology Student Association (TSA)
▸ Business Professionals of America (BPA)
▸ Health Occupations Students of America (HOSA)
▸ National Postsecondary Agricultural Student Organization (PAS)
▸ National Young Farmer Educational Association (NYFEA)

▸ **FFA**

> National FFA Organization
> 6060 FFA Drive
> PO Box 68960
> Indianapolis, IN 46268
> 317-802-6060
> www.ffa.org

Strategies: The FFA's official strategies are to:

1. Develop competent and assertive agricultural leadership.
2. Increase awareness of the global and technical importance of agriculture and its contribution to our well-being.
3. Strengthen the confidence of agriculture students in themselves and their work.
4. Promote the intelligent choice and establishment of an agricultural career.
5. Encourage achievement in supervised agricultural experience programs.
6. Encourage wise management of economic, environmental, and human resources of the community.
7. Develop interpersonal skills in teamwork, communications, human relations, and social interaction.
8. Build character and promote citizenship, volunteerism, and patriotism.

9. Promote cooperation and cooperative attitudes among all people.
10. Promote healthy life-styles.
11. Encourage excellence in scholarship.

Colors: The official colors used by the FFA are national blue and corn gold.

Motto: "Learning To Do, Doing to Learn, Earning to Live, Living to Serve."

Emblem: The national FFA emblem consists of five symbols, and is representative of the history, goals, and future of the organization. As a whole, the emblem represents the broad spectrum of FFA and agriculture. Each element within the emblem has unique significance:

▸ A cross-section of an ear of corn provides the foundation of the emblem, just as corn has historically served as the foundation crop of American agriculture. It is also a symbol of unity, as corn is grown in every state of the nation.

▸ A rising sun signifies progress, and holds a promise that tomorrow will bring a new day glowing with opportunity.

▸ A plow signifies labor and tillage of the soil, the backbone of agriculture and the historic foundation of our country's strength.

▸ An eagle, a national symbol, which, serves as a reminder of our freedom and ability to explore new horizons for the future of agriculture.

▸ An owl, long recognized for its wisdom, symbolizes the knowledge required to be successful in the agricultural industry.

In addition, the words "Agricultural Education" and the letters "FFA" are inscribed in the center to signify that a combination of learning and leadership is necessary for progressive agriculture.

Creed: "I believe in the future of agriculture, with a faith born not of words but of deeds – achievements won by the present and past generations of agriculturists; in the promise of better days through better ways, even as the better things we now enjoy have come to us from the struggles of former years.

"I believe that to live and work on a good farm, or to be engaged in other agricultural pursuits, is pleasant as well as challenging; for I know the joys and discomforts of agricultural life and hold an inborn fondness for those associations which, even in hours of discouragement, I cannot deny.

"I believe in leadership from ourselves and respect from others. I believe in my own ability to work efficiently and think clearly, with such knowledge and skill as I can secure, and in the ability of progressive agriculturists to serve our own and the public interest in producing and marketing the product of our toil.

"I believe in less dependence on begging and more power in bargaining; in the life abundant and enough honest wealth to help make it so – for others as well as myself; in less need for charity and more of it when needed; in being happy myself and playing square with those whose happiness depends upon me.

"I believe that American agriculture can and will hold true to the best traditions of our national life, and that I can exert an influence in my home and community which will stand solid for my part in that inspiring task."

National publications: New Horizons, FFA's official magazine, is published six times a year and distributed to affiliated members. The national organization publishes a variety of other resource materials for members and leaders.

▶ **Future Business Leaders of America – Phi Beta Lambda (FBLA – PBL)**

Future Business Leaders of America – Phi Beta Lambda (FBLA – PBL)
1912 Association Drive
Reston, VA 20191
800-325-2946
www.fbla-pbl.org
general@fbla.org

Goals: FBLA – PBL's official goals are to:

1. Develop capable, aggressive business leadership.
2. Strengthen the confidence of students in themselves and their work.
3. Create more interest in and understanding of American business enterprise.
4. Encourage members in the development of individual projects which contribute to the improvement of home, business, and community.
5. Develop character, prepare for useful citizenship, and foster patriotism.
6. Encourage and practice efficient money management.
7. Encourage scholarship and promote school loyalty.
8. Assist students in the establishment of occupational goals.
9. Facilitate the transition from school to work.

Colors: The official colors used by FBLA – PBL are blue and gold.

Emblem: The FBLA – PBL emblem depicts two flowing red ribbons emerging diagonally upwards and to the right from a field of blue. Beneath it and to the right, horizontally, are the English letters FBLA, a dot, and the Greek letters phi, beta, and lambda.

Creed: "I believe that education is the right of every person.

"I believe the future depends upon mutual understanding and cooperation among business, industry, labor, religious, family and educational institutions, as well as people around the world. I agree to do my utmost to bring about better understanding and cooperation among of all these groups.

"I believe every person should prepare for a useful occupation and should carry on that occupation in a manner that brings the greatest good to the greatest number.

"I believe every person should actively work toward improving social, political, community, and family life.

"I believe every person has the right to earn a living at a useful occupation and that this right should not be denied because of race, color, creed, sex, or handicap.

"I believe every person should take responsibility for carrying out assigned tasks in a manner that will brings credit to self, associates, school, and community.

" I believe I have the responsibility to work efficiently and think clearly, and I promise myself to use my abilities to make the world a better place for everyone."

National publications: Tomorrow's Business Leader goes to FBLA and FBLA Middle Level students; *Advisers' Hotline* to high school teachers; *Middle Level Advisers' Hotline* to Middle Level teachers; *Business Leader* to PBL members and advisers; and *The Professional Edge* to Professional Division members. All are published three times a year.

▸   **Family, Career and Community Leaders of America (FCCLA)**

Family, Career and Community Leaders of America (FCCLA), Inc.
1910 Association Drive
Reston, VA 20791-1584
703-476-4900
www.fcclainc.org

Purposes: FCCLA's official purposes are:

1.   To provide opportunities for personal development and preparation for adult life.
2.   To strengthen the function of the family as a unit of society.
3.   To encourage democracy through cooperative action in the home and community.
4.   To encourage individual and group involvement in helping achieve global cooperation and harmony.
5.   To promote greater understanding between youth and adults.
6.   To provide opportunities for making decisions and for assuming responsibilities.
7.   To prepare for the multiple roles of men and women in today's society.
8.   To promote family and consumer sciences and related occupations.

Emblem: The organization's emblem depicts the letters "FCCLA" in a bold "collegiate" typeface, surrounded by an oval featuring an arrowhead pointing upward and to the right. Inset within the oval are the words "Family, Career and Community Leaders of America". The collegiate lettering articulates a focus on education and student leadership. The swooping arrow arch represents an active organization that moves toward new arenas. The emblem is red, the color of the rose as a sign of strength, on a white background.

Creed: "We are the Family, Career and Community Leaders of America. We face the future with warm courage and high hope.

"For we have the clear consciousness of seeking old and precious values. For we are the builders of homes; homes for America's future; homes where living will be the expression of everything that is good and fair; homes where truth and love and security and faith will be realities, not dreams.

"We are the Family, Career and Community Leaders of America. We face the future with warm courage and high hope."

National publications: Teen Times, the official magazine of FCCLA, is published quarterly during the school year and distributed to affiliated members. *The Adviser*, published twice a year, is the official publication for FCCLA advisers. The national staff also publishes a variety of other resource materials for members and adult leaders. A free publication catalog is available upon request.

▸ DECA

DECA
1908 Association Drive
Reston, VA 20191
703-860-5000
www.deca.org

Goals: DECA's official goals are to:

1. Prepare marketing education students to take their proper places in the business   world.
2. Develop leadership characteristics.
3. Develop self-confidence and self-acceptance.
4. Develop a greater understanding of our competitive, free enterprise system.
5. Further develop occupational competencies needed for careers in marketing, management, and entrepreneurship.
6. Develop high ethical standards in personal and business relationships.
7. Develop effective international relationships.
8. Develop a greater awareness of career opportunities in marketing.
9. Develop greater proficiency in communication.
10. Develop greater appreciation of the responsibilities of citizenship.
11. Develop a healthy competitive spirit.
12. Develop social and business etiquette

Colors: The official colors used by DECA are blue and gold.

Emblem: The DECA emblem features a stylized diamond device with ten horizontal lines radiating through bold italic letters spelling "DECA". Beneath is the organizational descriptors," An Association of Marketing Students". The diamond is a modernized version of the original DECA diamond logo. Its four corners symbolize vocational understanding, civic consciousness, social intelligence, and leadership development. The radiating horizontal lines represent the organization's forward-looking attitude.

Creed: "I believe in the future which I am planning for myself in the field of marketing and management, and in the opportunities which my vocation offers.

"I believe in fulfilling the highest measure of service to my vocation, my fellow beings, my country and my God – that by so doing, I will be rewarded with personal satisfaction and material wealth.

"I believe in the democratic philosophies of private enterprise and competition, and in the freedoms of this nation – that these philosophies allow for the fullest development of my individual abilities.

"I believe that by doing my best to live according to these high principles, I will be of greater service both to myself and to mankind."

National publications: **DECA dimensions** is the official membership magazine, published four times during the school year. ***The Advisor*** newsletter provides timely information and teaching aids for chapter advisors, and is published seven times during the school year. The ***DECA Guide*** is an annual publication containing the official DECA Competitive Events Program guidelines.

▸ **SkillsUSA**

SkillsUSA
PO Box 3000
Leesburg, VA 20177-0300
703-777-8810
www.skillsusa.org

Purposes: SkillsUSA's official purposes are to:

▸ Unite in a common bond without regard to race, sex, religion, creed, or national origin, full-time students enrolled in classes with vocational trade, industrial, technological, and health occupation objectives.
▸ Provide leadership for the state organizations.
▸ Provide a clearinghouse for information and activities.
▸ Provide national recognition and prestige through an association and affiliated organizations.
▸ Provide a vehicle, national in scope, for organizations to work articulately with trade, industrial, technology and health occupations student groups.
▸ Develop leadership abilities through participation in educational, vocational, civic, recreational, and social activities.
▸ Foster a deep respect for the dignity of work.
▸ Assist students in establishing realistic vocational goals.
▸ Help students attain a purposeful life.
▸ Create enthusiasm for learning.
▸ Promote high standards in trade, ethics, workmanship, scholarship, and safety.
▸ Develop the ability of students to plan together, organize, and carry out worthy activities and projects through the use of the democratic process.
▸ Foster a wholesome understanding of the functions of labor and management organizations and a recognition of their mutual interdependence.
▸ Create among students, faculty members, patrons of the school, and persons in industry a sincere interest in and esteem for trade, industrial, technology, and health occupations education.
▸ Develop patriotism through a knowledge of our nation's heritage and the practice of democracy.
▸ Emphasize the importance of continuous education consistent to the needs of the individual and the requirements of his or her chosen occupation.

Colors: The official colors used by SkillsUSA are red, white, blue, and gold.

Emblem: The national SkillsUSA emblem consists of five symbols, and is representative of the history, goals, and future of the organization. Each element within the emblem has unique significance:

- The shield represents patriotism, and denotes belief in democracy, liberty, and the American way of life.
- The gear, symbolic of the industrial society, denotes the interdependence and cooperation of the individual working with labor and management for the betterment of mankind.
- The torch reflects the light of knowledge, which dispels the darkness of ignorance. In the light of the torch, progress will be made toward the vocational goals of the individual.
- The orbital circles present the challenge of modern technology and the training needed to accept and master the challenge of new technical frontiers and the need for continuous education.
- The hands represent the individual, and portray a search for knowledge and the desire to acquire a skill. In the process of attaining knowledge and skill, members develop a respect for the dignity of work and become productive and responsible citizens.

Pledge: "Upon my honor, I pledge:

"To prepare myself by diligent study and ardent practice to become a worker whose services will be recognized as honorable by my employer and fellow workers.

"To base my expectations of reward upon the solid foundation of service.

"To honor and respect my vocation in such a way as to bring repute to myself.

"And further, to spare no effort in upholding the ideals of SkillsUSA."

Creed: "I believe in the dignity of work. I hold that society has advanced to its present culture through the use of the individuals hands and mind. I will maintain a feeling of humbleness for the knowledge and skills that I receive from professionals, and I will conduct myself with dignity in the work I do.

"I believe in the American way of life. I know our culture is the result of freedom of action and opportunities won by the founders of our American republic, and I will uphold their ideals.

"I believe in education. I will endeavor to make the best use of knowledge, skills, and experience that I will learn in order that I may be a better leader in my chosen career and a better citizen in my community. To this end, I will continue my learning now and in the future.

"I believe in fair play. I will, through honesty and fair play, respect the rights of others. I will always conduct myself in the manner of the best professionals in my career and treat those with whom I work as I would like to be treated.

"I believe satisfaction is achieved by good work. I feel that compensation and personal satisfaction received for my work and services will be in proportion to my creative and productive ability.

"I believe in high moral and spiritual standards. I will endeavor to conduct myself in such a manner as to set an example for others by living a wholesome life and by fulfilling my responsibilities as a citizen of my community."

National publications: SkillsUSA Champions is the official membership magazine, published quarterly.

▶ **Technology Student Association (TSA)**

Technology Student Association (TSA)
1914 Association Drive
Reston, VA 20191-1540
703-860-9000
www.tsaweb.org

Purposes: TSA's general purposes are to:

▶ Assist state delegations in the growth and development of TSA.
▶ Assist state delegations in the development and leadership in social, economic, educational, and community activities.
▶ Increase the knowledge and understanding of our technological world.
▶ Assist technology education students in the making of informed and meaningful career goals.

TSA's specific purposes are to:

▶ Develop, through individual and teamwork, the ability of members to plan, organize, and use a variety of resources to solve problems.
▶ Explore technology and develop an understanding of technological literacy.
▶ Promote high standards of learning through curricular resource activities.
▶ Encourage students in expressing creativity.
▶ Develop consumer awareness.
▶ Provide career opportunity information pertaining to a broad range of occupations, including training requisites, working conditions, salaries, or wages, and other relevant information.
▶ Provide exploratory experiences in classrooms and laboratories, and develop partnerships in business or industry to acquaint students with career opportunities.
▶ Assist in providing guidance and counseling for students enrolled in technology education programs in making informed and meaningful career choices.
▶ Expose students to the responsibility of representing a large membership.
▶ Instill desirable work habits and attitudes toward the positive way of life in students and foster a deep respect for the dignity of work.
▶ Prepare individuals for enrollment in advanced or highly skilled vocational and technical education programs.

Colors: The official colors used by TSA are scarlet, white, and blue.

Motto: "Learning to live in a technical world."

Emblem: The TSA emblem is a rectangular shape containing the letters "TSA" in large, stylized print. The letters are white on a blue background. Above these letters is a red rectangle; below these letters are the words "Technology Student Association" in white letters on a red background.

Creed: "I believe that Technology Education holds an important place in my life in the technical world. I believe there is a need for the development of good attitudes concerning work, tools, materials, experimentation, and processes of industry.

"Guided by my teachers, artisans from industry, and my own initiative, I will strive to do my best in making my school, community, state, and nation better places in which to live.

"I will accept the responsibilities that are mine. I will accept the theories that are supported by proper evidence. I will explore on my own for safer, more effective methods of working and living.

"I will strive to develop a cooperative attitude and will exercise tact and respect for other individuals.

"Through the work of my hands and mind, I will express my ideas to the best of my ability.

"I will make it my goal to do better each day the task before me, and to be steadfast in my belief in my God, and my fellow Americans."

National publications: School Scene is TSA's member magazine, published three times yearly. TSA provides a Program Kit with operational information for chapters; an annual Information Directory; official TSA Competitive Events Guides for high school and middle school; and *The Great Technology Adventure*, a guide for elementary level teachers.

▶ Business Professionals of America (BPA)

Business Professionals of America (BPA)
National Center
5454 Cleveland Avenue
Columbus, OH 43231-4021
800-334-2007
www.bpa.org

Purposes: BPA's official purposes are to:

▸ Develop student leadership.
▸ Promote better understanding at local, state, and national levels.
▸ Improve poise, sociability, attitude, and tact.
▸ Develop competence in business and office occupations.
▸ Promote student ambition for useful purposes.
▸ Learn to plan effectively.
▸ Develop an enthusiasm for learning and for remaining knowledgeable in the business and office fields.
▸ Develop confidence and a spirit of competition.
▸ Learn to get along with others.
▸ Develop loyalty through *esprit de corps*.
▸ Understand and promote business.

Colors: The official colors used by BPA are navy blue, tan, and red.

Logo: The BPA logo is a graphic representation of the organization's name. The slogan "Today's students, Tomorrow's business professions" always appears near the logo. An organizational shield is used for ceremonial purposes only, and is not depicted in the Handbook.

Pledge: "We are met in a spirit of friendship and goodwill as we prepare for productive lives in business and office careers. We work together to develop professionalism and leadership through Business Professionals of America, and pledge our loyalty to our nation."

National publications: Communiqué is BPA's official magazine, published four times a year and distributed to each member.

▶ Health Occupations Students of America

Health Occupations Students of America, Inc.
6021 Morriss Road, Suite 111
Flower Mound, TX 75028
800-321-HOSA (4672)
www.hosa.org

Purposes: HOSA's official purpose is to develop leadership and technical HOSA skill competencies through a program of motivation, awareness, and recognition, which is an integral part of the Health Science Technology Education instruction program. The goals that HOSA believes are vital to each member are to:

- ▶ Promote physical, mental, and social well-being.
- ▶ Develop effective leadership qualities and skills.
- ▶ Develop the ability to communicate more effectively with people.
- ▶ Develop character.
- ▶ Develop responsible citizenship traits.
- ▶ Understand the importance of pleasing oneself as well as being of service to others.
- ▶ Build self-confidence and pride in one's work.
- ▶ Make realistic career choices and seek successful employment in the health-care field.
- ▶ Develop an understanding of the importance in interacting and cooperating with other students and organizations.
- ▶ Encourage individual and group achievement.
- ▶ Develop an understanding of current health-care issues, environmental concerns, and survival needs of the community, the nation, and the world.
- ▶ Encourage involvement in local, state, and national health-care and education projects.
- ▶ Support Health Care Technology instructional objectives.
- ▶ Promote career opportunities in Health Care.

Colors: The colors of HOSA are navy blue, maroon, and medical white.

Motto: "The Hands of HOSA Mold the Health of Tomorrow."

Symbol: HOSA's symbol shows a navy blue triangle, containing (in white) a pair of hands on either side of a human figure above the letters "HOSA" in block script. The triangle is above the words "Founded 1976" in navy blue block script in an arc. A maroon circle that contains the words "HEALTH OCCUPATIONS STUDENTS OF AMERICA" in white block script surrounds these. The circle represents the continuity of health care. The triangle represents the three aspects of humankind well being: social, physical, and mental. The hands signify the caring of each HOSA member.

Creed: "I believe in the health care profession.

"I believe in the profession for which I am being trained, and in the opportunities that my training offers.

"I believe in education.

"I believe that through education I will be able to make the greatest use of my skills, knowledge, and experience in order to become a contributing member of the health care team and of my community.

"I believe in myself.

"I believe that, by using the knowledge and skills of my profession, I will become more aware of myself. Through fulfilling these goals I will become a more responsible citizen.

"I believe that each individual is important in his or her own right; therefore, I will treat each person with respect and love.

"To this end, I dedicate my training, my skills, and myself to serve others through Health Occupations Students of America."

National publications: *HOSA Magazine* is provided in electronic format and posted twice annually. It can be viewed at www.hosa.org.

▶ **National Postsecondary Agricultural Student Organization (PAS)**

National Postsecondary Agricultural Student Organization (PAS)
6060 FFA Drive, PO Box 68960
Indianapolis, IN 46268-0960
317-802-4214
www.nationalpas.org

Purpose and values: The purpose of the National Postsecondary Agricultural Student Organization (PAS) is to provide an opportunities for members to develop the skills and abilities needed to enter and advance in careers in agriculture, agribusiness, horticulture, and natural resources.

The organization's values are:

▶ Developing individual leadership abilities.
▶ Promoting intellectual growth.
▶ Developing technical competencies.
▶ Fostering strong personal ethics.
▶ Encouraging life-long learning.
▶ Recognizing a synergy exists in diversity.
▶ Uniting education and industry.

Motto: "Uniting Education and Industry in Agriculture."

Symbol: The organizational symbol depicts the letters "PAS" in bold font in an oval.

▸ **National Young Farmer Educational Association (NYFEA)**

National Young Farmer Educational Association (NYFEA)
PO Box 20326
Montgomery, AL 36120
334-288-0097
www.nyfea.org

Purpose and vision: The purpose of the NYFEA is to develop leaders, inspire service, strengthen communities, and enhance the success potential for American agriculture, especially the beginning farmers. The vision of the NYFEA is a world where all people value and understand the vital role of agriculture, food, fiber, and natural resource systems in advancing personal and global well being.

The core goals of NYFEA are to:

▸ Provide quality products that are perceived by members, advisors, teachers, and educational and business partners as adding value to lives of NYFEA members.
▸ Continually build human resources through a highly motivated, committed national board, national officers, national delegate assembly, and national staff.
▸ Build and maintain a solid delivery system.
▸ Build a customer base that includes all people involved in agriculture, food, fiber, and natural resource systems.
▸ Establish and maintain a secure financial base.

Logo: The organization's logo shows the letters "nyfea" in white font inside a dark rectangle. To the left is a circular device that contains two drop-like symbols and a vertical oval divided by a white line. Beneath all are the words "The Association for EDUCATING AGRICULTURAL LEADERS".

National publications: The ***Leader for Agriculture*** is published intermittently and sent to each NYFEA member, the corporate community, prospective young farmers, and agricultural leaders. The ***Young Farmer and Ag Leaders UPDATE*** is printed at least four times annually and provides current leadership information to NYFEA members. Both are available online at www.nyfea.org.

APPENDIX III
Specific Duties and Responsibilities for Each CTSO Student Officer

▶ **Duties of the President**

The President's job is one of organization and leadership. He or she is a leader and manager, seeing to it that the organization meets the goals of future years. Specific duties include:

▶ Knowing the group members and their abilities; involving as many members in various activities as possible.
▶ Keeping the organization moving in an enthusiastic manner, encouraging others to become interested.
▶ Coordinating efforts by keeping in touch with all officers, members, and advisors.
▶ Making contacts with speakers or guests for organizational meetings well in advance, by phone or letter. Following up with a thank-you note by mail. (This may be delegated to the Secretary.)
▶ Presiding over and conducting meetings according to parliamentary procedure.
▶ Keeping members on the subject and within time limits at all meetings.
▶ Introducing guests and recognizing special arrangements at all meetings.
▶ Representing the organization at special functions and events; speaking at various functions as requested, always portraying the thoughts of the membership.
▶ Calling special organization meetings or special officer meetings, and appointing committees when required.

▶ **Duties of the Vice-President**

The Vice-President's job is to assist the President whenever needed, be ready to take over for the President if necessary, and ensure that committees function properly. Specific duties include:

▶ Setting up committee schedules with each chairperson; ensuring that committee worksheets are completed and the information transferred to the master copy.
▶ Reviewing committee programs with the executive committee; ensuring that all dates are listed on the organizational calendar and all contacts made for publicity.
▶ Meeting with committees and promoting action; coordinating with chairpersons to secure speakers and other meeting information.
▶ Ensuring that committee reports are prepared after each meeting and submitted to the secretary; making sure that blank reporting forms are available for distribution.
▶ Maintaining a working knowledge of parliamentary procedure.
▶ Helping the President develop a program agenda.

▶ Duties of the Secretary

The Secretary should be aware of all chapter and committee actions. He or she should receive an accurate accounting of all necessary information about past meetings. Specific duties include:

▶ Preparing and reading the minutes of all meetings.

▶ Maintaining a list of all official business to be conducted during the meeting; providing this list to the President.

▶ Completing all official chapter correspondence (e.g., e-mails, invitations, formal announcements, thank-you notes, and letters).

▶ Counting and recording all votes during meetings.

▶ Ensuring that the following information is on hand for each meeting:
  – Copies of committee reports.
  – Minutes from previous meetings.
  – Local constitution and by-laws.
  – Local, state, and national programs of activities.

▶ Keeping accurate reports to send to state and national offices on or before due dates.

▶ Maintaining an accurate membership roll; preparing the membership roster for payment of state and national dues.

▶ Maintaining an accurate history of the chapter (this may be delegated to the historian).

▶ Duties of the Treasurer

The Treasurer's job is to handle chapter funds, keep accurate financial records, and stay up-to-date on all necessary expenditures. Specific duties include:

▶ Keeping an accurate record of all receipts and expenditures.

▶ Carrying all funds to and from the point of deposit.

▶ Reporting all expenditures at each meeting.

▶ Following approved school procedures for paying expenses and keeping financial records.

▶ Assisting the secretary with maintaining membership rolls and preparing rosters.

▶ Preparing budgets.

▶ Duties of the Reporter

The Reporter is responsible for linking with the community. Specific duties include:

▶ Sending news and pictures to local newspapers, television and radio stations, and community access TV ("local access cable") regarding upcoming local, state, and national events.

▶ Maintaining a chapter website.

▶ Maintaining a chapter scrapbook.

▶ Taking photos of chapter events; arranging services of a professional photographer if needed.

▶ Working closely with the public relations committee and the community.

▶ Duties of the Sentinel or Sergeant-At-Arms

The Sentinel or Sergeant-At-Arms is responsible for handling details properly and efficiently during a meeting. Specific duties include:

- Caring for all organizational equipment and accouterments used for meetings and ceremonies.
- Welcoming visitors and friends of the organization.
- Assisting the President in maintaining order.
- Providing refreshments and entertainment.
- Setting up the site for meetings and assemblies.
- Ensuring that the site is comfortable for all.

▶ Duties of the Parliamentarian

The Parliamentarian's job is to ensure that rules of order are followed during meetings. Duties include:

- Answering questions about correct use of parliamentary procedure.
- Ensuring that a copy of ***Robert's Rules of Order*** or other recognized parliamentary procedure resource is available at all meetings.
- Working closely with the Sentinel/Sergeant-At-Arms and other officers to ensure that meetings are conducted in an organized manner.
- Reviewing the agenda prior to the start of the meeting.
- Ensuring that the rights of each individual are respected.
- Ensuring that the will of the majority is carried out, and that the rights of the minority are preserved.

NOTES

APPENDIX IV
The "Top Fifty"
A List of Leadership and Personal Development Publications

1. Bennis, W. (2003). *On becoming a leader: The leadership classic.* Cambridge, MA: Perseus Publishing.
2. Bennis, W. & Biederman, P. W. (1998). *Organizing genius: the secrets of creative collaboration.* Cambridge, MA: Perseus Publishing.
3. Berne, E. (1964). *Games People Play: The basic handbook of transactional analysis.* New York, NY: Random House.
4. Block, P. (1993). *Stewardship: Choosing service over self-interest.* San Francisco, CA: Berett-Koehler Publishers, Inc.
5. Buckingham, M. & Clifton, D. O. (2001). *Now discover your strengths.* New York, NY: TheFree Press.
6. Canfield, J. H. (2000). T*he power of focus.* Deerfield Beach, FL: Health Communications, Inc.
7. Carnegie, D. (1956). How to develop self-confidence and influence people by public speaking. New York, NY: Simon & Schuster.
8. Carnegie, D. (1948). *How to stop worrying and start living.* New York, NY: Simon & Schuster.
9. Carnegie, D. (1936). *How to win friends and influence people.* New York, NY: Simon & Schuster.
10. Carnegie, D. (1962). *The quick and easy way to effective public speaking.* New York, NY: Simon & Schuster.
11. Christopher, E. & Smith, L. (1987). *Leadership training through gaming: Power, people, and problem solving.* New York, NY: Nichols Publishing Company.
12. Clifton, D. & Nelson, P. (1992). *Soar with your strengths.* New York, NY: Dell Publishing.
13. Covey, S. (1998). *The seven habits of highly effective teens: The ultimate teenage success guide.* New York, NY: Simon & Schuster.
14. Covey, S. R. (1990). *The seven habits of highly effective people.* New York, NY: Simon & Schuster.
15. Depree, M. (1989). *Leadership is an art.* New York, NY: Dell Publishing.
16. Depree, M. (1992). *Leadership jazz.* New York, NY: Dell Publishing.
17. Dunbar, S. (2001). *Parliamentary procedure made easy.* http://parlipro.northwest.net/.
18. Fritz, S. (2005). *Interpersonal skills for leadership* (2nd ed.). Upper Saddle River, NJ: Pearson Prentice Hall.
19. Greenleaf, R. K., Spears, L. C. & Covey, S. R. (1991). *Servant leadership: A journey into the nature of legitimate power and greatness.* Mahwah, NJ: Paulist Press.
20. Harper, J. K. (2002). *The meeting will please come to order.* Kenwood, CA: Oak Point Press.
21. Hegarty, E. J. (1981 revised). *How to run better meetings.* Melbourne, FL: Kreiger Publishing.
22. Henry, L. C. (1984 revised). *Best quotations for all occasions.* Greenwich, CN: Fawcett Books.
23. Hill, N. & Stone, W. C. (1977). *Success through a positive mental attitude.* Englewood Cliffs, NJ: Prentice-Hall.
24. Jones, O. G. (1971). *Parliamentary procedure at a glance.* New York, NY: Hawthorn Books, Inc.
25. Klein, A. (2000). The change-your-life quote book. New York, NY: Gramercy Books.
26. Kouzes, J. M. & Posner, B. Z. (2003, revised) *Credibility: Why people gain and lose it, why people demand it.* San Francisco, CA: Jossey-Bass Inc.

27. Kouzes, J. M. & Posner, B. Z. (1995). *The leadership challenge*. San Francisco, CA: Jossey-Bass Inc.
28. Lindsell-Roberts, S. (2004). *Strategic business letters and e-mail*. Boston, MA: Houghton Mifflin.
29. Maxwell, J. (2003 revised). *Developing the leaders around you*. Nashville, TN: Thomas Nelson, Inc.
30. Maxwell, J. (1993). *Developing the leader within you*. Nashville, TN: Thomas Nelson, Inc.
31. Maxwell, J. (1999). *The 21 indispensable qualities of a leader: Becoming the person others will want to follow*. Nashville, TN: Thomas Nelson, Inc.
32. Maxwell, J. (2001). *The 17 indisputable laws of teamwork: Embrace them and empower your team*. Nashville, TN: Thomas Nelson, Inc.
33. Maxwell, J. (2003). *Leadership 101: What every leader needs to know*. Nashville, TN: Thomas Nelson, Inc.
34. MacGregor, M. G. (1999). *Designing student leadership programs: Transforming the leadership potential of youth*. Morrison, CO: youthleadership.com.
35. Mackenzie, A. (1989). *Time for success: A goal-getter's strategy*. New York, NY: McGraw-Hill Publishers.
36. Mitchell, M. & Corr, J. (2000). *Complete idiot's guide to etiquette*. New York, NY: Alpha Books.
37. Official chapter activity and/or advisors' guide, available from each respective CTSO.
38. Official student manual and/or student handbook, available from each respective CTSO.
39. Palmer, P. J. (1997). *The courage to teach: Exploring the inner landscape of a teacher's life*. San Francisco, CA: Jossey-Bass.
40. Peale, N. V. (1967). *Enthusiasm makes the difference*. Englewood Cliffs, NJ: Prentice-Hall.
41. Peale, N. V. (1956). *The power of positive thinking*. New York, NY: Prentice-Hall.
42. Ricketts, C. (2003). *Leadership: Personal development and career success*. Albany, NY: Delmar Publishers.
43. Robert, H. M. III; Evans, W. J.; Honemann, D. H.; & Balch, T. J. (2000). *Robert's rules of order: newly revised* (10th ed.). New York, NY: Perseus Publishing.
44. Safire, W. & Safir, L. (1990). *Leadership: A treasury of great quotations for everybody who aspires to be a leader*. New York, NY: Simon & Schuster.
45. Stewart, M.; Lee, J. S.; Hunter, S.; Scheil, B.; Fraze, S. D.; & Terry, R. (2004). *Developing leadership and communication skills*. Upper Saddle River, NJ: Pearson Prentice Hall.
46. Sturgis, Alice (2000). *Standard code of parliamentary procedure* (4th edition). New York, NY: McGraw-Hill Book Company.
47. van Linden, J. A. & Fertman, C. I. (1983). *Youth leadership: A guide to understanding leadership development in adolescents*. San Francisco, CA: Jossey-Bass Inc.
48. Waitley, D. E. (1984). *Seeds of greatness*. New York, NY: Simon & Schuster.
49. Zigler, Z. (1979). *See you at the top*. Gretna, LA: Pelican Publications.
50. Zigler, Z. (1986). *Top performance: How to develop excellence in yourself & others*. New York, NY: Berkley Books.

a. Evaluating the Public Relations Program

Directions: Pease read each of the following statements. Decide which rating is most appropriate concerning the organization and its efforts this year.

	N/A	Good	Fair	Poor
All members have read and studied the Code of Ethics.............................	☐	☐	☐	☐
All members have receive instructions on presenting a good image............	☐	☐	☐	☐
Official dress was worn when appropriate...	☐	☐	☐	☐
All member wore uniforms to organizational functions..............................	☐	☐	☐	☐
The advisors dressed neatly and used good personal hygiene......................	☐	☐	☐	☐
At least one committee was responsible for public relations.......................	☐	☐	☐	☐
Counselors and other teachers were presented information on the organization..	☐	☐	☐	☐
Individuals inside the organization were recognized (or awarded) for efforts on behalf of the group..	☐	☐	☐	☐
Individuals outside the organization were recognized (or awarded) for efforts on behalf of the group..	☐	☐	☐	☐
Key community groups and individuals were identified..............................	☐	☐	☐	☐
Members made presentations at community meetings.................................	☐	☐	☐	☐
Community organizations and members were invited to make presentations to the student organization...	☐	☐	☐	☐
Activities were well advertised...	☐	☐	☐	☐
Open house was conducted...	☐	☐	☐	☐
A banquet or other award program was conducted......................................	☐	☐	☐	☐
Activities were conducted during designated days or weeks........................	☐	☐	☐	☐
Service and educator activities were conducted..	☐	☐	☐	☐
Newspapers were used to publicize the organization..................................	☐	☐	☐	☐
Radio was used to publicize organization..	☐	☐	☐	☐

a. Evaluating the Public Relations Program (continued)

Directions: Please read each of the following statements. Decide which rating is most appropriate concerning the organization and its efforts this year.

	N/A	Good	Fair	Poor
The internet was used to publicize the organization.....................................	☐	☐	☐	☐
Television was used to publicize the organization......................................	☐	☐	☐	☐
Community groups agreed to assist the organization..................................	☐	☐	☐	☐
School administrators assisted the organization...	☐	☐	☐	☐
Counselors and other teachers had a positive and helpful attitude...............	☐	☐	☐	☐
Other students had a positive attitude toward the student organization...	☐	☐	☐	☐

b. Evaluating the Financial Operation of the Organization

Directions: Please read each of the following statements. Decide which rating is most appropriate concerning the organization and its efforts this year.

	N/A	Good	Fair	Poor
The budget:				
is in written form	☐	☐	☐	☐
excludes departmental operations	☐	☐	☐	☐
includes activities related to organizational goals	☐	☐	☐	☐
was developed at the beginning of organizational year	☐	☐	☐	☐
was developed by students	☐	☐	☐	☐
was developed under advisor guidance	☐	☐	☐	☐
was developed using member ideas	☐	☐	☐	☐
was approved by the organization	☐	☐	☐	☐
was approved by school administration	☐	☐	☐	☐
includes memberships dues as income	☐	☐	☐	☐
includes all fund-raising activities as expected income	☐	☐	☐	☐
includes each fund-raising activity as a separate entry	☐	☐	☐	☐
includes each expense as a separate listing	☐	☐	☐	☐
includes each activity planned by the organization	☐	☐	☐	☐
is included with organization's plan of activities	☐	☐	☐	☐
is on file with the administration	☐	☐	☐	☐
has provisions for periodic checks for income and expenses	☐	☐	☐	☐
Dues were collected and recorded	☐	☐	☐	☐
All members paid dues	☐	☐	☐	☐
Appropriate fund-raising activities were conducted	☐	☐	☐	☐
Receipts and/or multiple carbons were used to keeps records of financial transactions	☐	☐	☐	☐
Materials were ordered according to school policy	☐	☐	☐	☐
A copy of orders was kept on file	☐	☐	☐	☐

b. Evaluating the Financial Operation of the Organization (continued)

Directions: Please read each of the following statements. Decide which rating is most appropriate concerning the organization and its efforts this year.

	N/A	Good	Fair	Poor
Fund-raising activities were planned by committees......................................	☐	☐	☐	☐
Fund-raising projects were consistent with organizational goals..................	☐	☐	☐	☐
Fund-raising activities were school approved...	☐	☐	☐	☐
Fund-raising activities were worthwhile and educational.............................	☐	☐	☐	☐
Fund-raising activities were effective in terms of effort and time expended...	☐	☐	☐	☐
All members were involved in fund-raising activities...................................	☐	☐	☐	☐
Fund-raising activities were scheduled on school calendar..........................	☐	☐	☐	☐
Funds were disbursed according to school policy...	☐	☐	☐	☐
Receipts were issued to keep track of finances...	☐	☐	☐	☐
Materials were ordered by following school policy......................................	☐	☐	☐	☐
Copies of all purchase transactions are kept on file.....................................	☐	☐	☐	☐

c. Evaluating the Participation of Special Needs Students

Directions: Please read each of the following statements. Decide which rating is most appropriate concerning the organization and its efforts this year.

	N/A	Good	Fair	Poor
A list of special needs students who could benefit from the organization in your local situation was developed............................	☐	☐	☐	☐
A counselor, special education teacher and/or administrator were involved in developing the above list................................	☐	☐	☐	☐
Attempts were made to get special needs students to join............................	☐	☐	☐	☐
Assemblies or other presentations were used to inform special needs students of the organization................................	☐	☐	☐	☐
Practical aspects of the organization were presented when providing information about the organization................................	☐	☐	☐	☐
Any special needs students already involved were enlisted for recruitment of others................................	☐	☐	☐	☐
Awards and public recognition were provided for special needs students................................	☐	☐	☐	☐
All members of the organization were asked for suggestions on recruitment of special needs students................................	☐	☐	☐	☐
Counselors, teachers, and administrators were involved in recruitment suggestions and efforts................................	☐	☐	☐	☐
Participation of special needs students were recorded............................	☐	☐	☐	☐
Leadership activities of special needs students participating were maintained................................	☐	☐	☐	☐
Necessary modifications were made in the organization's activities to allow for participation of special needs students............................	☐	☐	☐	☐
Professionals were asked for help in making needed modifications............	☐	☐	☐	☐
Students and advisor evaluated student progress at each level and necessary adjustments were made................................	☐	☐	☐	☐
The number of special needs students involved was recorded....................	☐	☐	☐	☐

c. Evaluating the Participation of Special Needs Students (continued)

Directions: Please read each of the following statements. Decide which rating is most appropriate concerning the organization and its efforts this year.

	N/A	Good	Fair	Poor
A goal was set for an increase in number of special needs students participating..	☐	☐	☐	☐
Students and counselors were informed concerning goals set.................	☐	☐	☐	☐
If strategies for including special needs students were not effective, they were changed...	☐	☐	☐	☐

d. Evaluating the Program of Activities

Directions: Please read each of the following statements. Decide which rating is most appropriate concerning the organization and its efforts the year.

	N/A	Good	Fair	Poor
The program of activities was a written plan...............................	☐	☐	☐	☐
The activities were challenging...	☐	☐	☐	☐
The activities were educational...	☐	☐	☐	☐
A majority of members participate in development......................	☐	☐	☐	☐
The program was discussed, reviewed and approved at a regular meeting...	☐	☐	☐	☐
The activities were designed to develop skills which make members more employable..	☐	☐	☐	☐
The activities were consistent with state and national objectives...	☐	☐	☐	☐
The program was realistic...	☐	☐	☐	☐
The program was developed early in the year............................	☐	☐	☐	☐
A committee was established for each major aspect of the organization......	☐	☐	☐	☐
Each committee planned activities..	☐	☐	☐	☐
The activities were completed...	☐	☐	☐	☐
Most members participated in each activity.............................	☐	☐	☐	☐
Cost of the activity was as planned......................................	☐	☐	☐	☐
The activity was worth the time and effort..............................	☐	☐	☐	☐
The activities planned were based on last year's program............	☐	☐	☐	☐
Administrative approval was obtained...................................	☐	☐	☐	☐
A standard format for planning activities was used by all committees.........	☐	☐	☐	☐
Costs involved were noted...	☐	☐	☐	☐

d. Evaluating the Program of Activities (continued)

Directions: Please read each of the following statements. Decide which rating is most appropriate concerning the organization and its efforts this year.

	N/A	Good	Fair	Poor
The format used answered the following:				
What will be done?..	☐	☐	☐	☐
When will activity occur?...	☐	☐	☐	☐
How many members will participate?..........................	☐	☐	☐	☐
Objectives and goals were included............................	☐	☐	☐	☐
The amount budgeted was included.............................	☐	☐	☐	☐
The program was printed...	☐	☐	☐	☐
Each member received a copy......................................	☐	☐	☐	☐
A monthly calendar of activities was prepared............	☐	☐	☐	☐

e. Evaluating Leadership and Personal Development

Directions: Please read each of the following statements. Decide which rating is most appropriate concerning the organization and its efforts this year.

	N/A	Good	Fair	Poor
A plan was developed for teaching leadership and personal development	☐	☐	☐	☐
Instruction on leadership and personal development was included in the classroom for activities	☐	☐	☐	☐
Instruction on social graces was offered	☐	☐	☐	☐
Activities and instruction were centered around working with others	☐	☐	☐	☐
Personality awareness was discussed by students and/or advisor	☐	☐	☐	☐
Instruction concerning citizenship was given	☐	☐	☐	☐
Communication was offered as a topic of importance	☐	☐	☐	☐
Money management was taught	☐	☐	☐	☐
The importance of committee membership was stressed	☐	☐	☐	☐
A variety of methods were used to include leadership and personal development in instruction	☐	☐	☐	☐
All students received instruction in leadership and personal development	☐	☐	☐	☐
A plan was developed for teaching parliamentary procedure	☐	☐	☐	☐
A plan was developed for teaching students how to prepare and present a speech	☐	☐	☐	☐
All students practiced giving some type of speech	☐	☐	☐	☐

f. Evaluating Local Officers

Directions: Please read each of the following statements. Decide which rating is most appropriate concerning the organization and its efforts this year.

	N/A	Good	Fair	Poor
All students were informed of duties and responsibilities of each office	☐	☐	☐	☐
Each member was encouraged to consider preparing for an office	☐	☐	☐	☐
Students established a nominating committee	☐	☐	☐	☐
A nominating committee was utilized	☐	☐	☐	☐
Students and advisor developed an application for each office	☐	☐	☐	☐
An application form was used for each office	☐	☐	☐	☐
Secret ballots were used	☐	☐	☐	☐
The advisor supervised elections	☐	☐	☐	☐
The nominating committee nominated at east two candidates	☐	☐	☐	☐
Nominations were allowed from the floor	☐	☐	☐	☐
Local officers successfully performed duties	☐	☐	☐	☐
The advisor assisted the officers throughout the year	☐	☐	☐	☐

g. Evaluating Participation in Activities

Directions: Please read each of the following statements. Decide which rating is most appropriate concerning the organization and its efforts this year.

	N/A	Good	Fair	Poor
Students were informed of available activities..	☐	☐	☐	☐
All students participated in some activity...	☐	☐	☐	☐
Appropriate activities were selected by the advisor and members................	☐	☐	☐	☐
Local competitive activities were established..	☐	☐	☐	☐
Students were prepared to participate in activities.......................................	☐	☐	☐	☐
Records were kept of organizational activities..	☐	☐	☐	☐
Records of individual participation were kept..	☐	☐	☐	☐
An objective procedure was established for selecting participants...............	☐	☐	☐	☐
An objective procedure was followed in selecting participants...................	☐	☐	☐	☐
Students were informed concerning the system for selection of participants..	☐	☐	☐	☐
Guidelines were developed for standards of member conduct when participating in activities...	☐	☐	☐	☐
Students were aware of standards of conduct..	☐	☐	☐	☐
Standards of conduct were followed during all activities............................	☐	☐	☐	☐
Arrangements for activities were made in advance.......................................	☐	☐	☐	☐
Constructive activities were provided for any free time during activities....	☐	☐	☐	☐
Students were always supervised during all activities..................................	☐	☐	☐	☐

h. Evaluating Award and Recognition Programs

Directions: Pease read each of the following statements. Decide which rating is most appropriate concerning the organization and its efforts this year.

	N/A	Good	Fair	Poor
Individuals received assistance in setting goals..	☐	☐	☐	☐
All deserving members were recognized..	☐	☐	☐	☐
Progress toward awards was monitored..	☐	☐	☐	☐
Individual awards programs were conducted...	☐	☐	☐	☐
Group awards were provided..	☐	☐	☐	☐
Achievement awards were established..	☐	☐	☐	☐
Proficiency awards were established..	☐	☐	☐	☐
Checklists of skills needed to receive awards were developed....................	☐	☐	☐	☐
Checklists were used in selecting award recipients....................................	☐	☐	☐	☐
Members were made aware of possible awards..	☐	☐	☐	☐
All promised awards were presented..	☐	☐	☐	☐
Each student worked toward at least one award..	☐	☐	☐	☐
A point system (or other objective method) was used for selecting award recipients...	☐	☐	☐	☐
High standards were maintained for awards...	☐	☐	☐	☐
The recognition event was properly planned	☐	☐	☐	☐
The event was enjoyable..	☐	☐	☐	☐
The event was smoothly conducted..	☐	☐	☐	☐
Many members were involved in conducting the event...............................	☐	☐	☐	☐
Speaking and presentation of awards by advisor was at a minimum during the event..	☐	☐	☐	☐

h. Evaluating Award and Recognition Programs (continued)

Directions: Please reach each of the following statements. Decide which rating is most appropriate concerning the organization and its efforts this year.

	N/A	Good	Fair	Poor
A script was developed and used for the event...	☐	☐	☐	☐
If a speaker was used, a time limit was given...	☐	☐	☐	☐
The event lasted no more than two hours...	☐	☐	☐	☐
Guests were treated properly..	☐	☐	☐	☐
The event began on time...	☐	☐	☐	☐
Entertainment, if used, was appropriate...	☐	☐	☐	☐

i. Evaluating Students' Advancement in the Organization

Directions: Please read each of the following statements. Decide which rating is most appropriate concerning the organization and its efforts this year.

	N/A	Good	Fair	Poor
All members were informed of requirements for degrees............................	☐	☐	☐	☐
Degree requirement lists were prepared and given to each member.............	☐	☐	☐	☐
Classroom time was scheduled on a regular basis to assist students with degree applications..	☐	☐	☐	☐
Every member developed plans for degree advancement............................	☐	☐	☐	☐
A degree file was kept on every student..	☐	☐	☐	☐
Most member attained local degrees (Note: Members and advisor may want to set a percentage.)......................	☐	☐	☐	☐
Every qualified student applied for an advanced degree..............................	☐	☐	☐	☐
Chapter officer conducted formal ceremonies recognizing individuals who received local degrees..	☐	☐	☐	☐
News articles were prepared to recognize individuals receiving degrees...	☐	☐	☐	☐
Certificates, pins, or other appropriate forms of recognition were presented to degree recipients during degree ceremonies...........................	☐	☐	☐	☐

NOTES

NOTES

INDEX

E

F

G

H

I

J

L

NOTES

NOTES